7.20.21
To Will,
God Bless!

2.0.2.

To Willi

God Bless !

Jun Lola

YOUR MORNING CUP OF
Inspiration

A Written Devotional from
Fearless Faith Ministries

Dan Wheeler, Terry Steen, Brian Roland

WESTBOW
PRESS®
A DIVISION OF THOMAS NELSON
& ZONDERVAN

WestBow Press books may be ordered through booksellers or by contacting:

WestBow Press
A Division of Thomas Nelson & Zondervan
1663 Liberty Drive
Bloomington, IN 47403
www.westbowpress.com
1 (866) 928-1240

All Scripture quotations are taken from the King James Version.

ISBN: 978-1-9736-8073-4 (sc)
ISBN: 978-1-9736-8072-7 (e)

Print information available on the last page.

WestBow Press rev. date: 12/06/2019

What People Are Saying!

"What an inspiration your messages have been. I've needed them so much."

Karin W

"They inspire me every day. So many life-giving examples especially since there's so much negativity in the world."

Lani H

"I am continually encouraged and uplifted by the daily devotions. Sometimes we just need an encouraging word and to be reminded of God's eternal love with no condemnation. Dan, Terry and Brian bring forth God's truth in a simple, loving and kind way.

Cheryl B

"This ministry gives short little devotionals that help anyone get through their day. Sometimes it is the uplifting you need for the moment, other times it is the thought that keeps you going. I am so thankful for Dan, Terry and Brian."

Edie B

"They are wholesome, genuine, regular guys just trying to be an encouragement to others. We all need to be better and encourage others."

Jean B

Introduction

Dan Wheeler was a popular on-air television host for QVC for twenty-nine years. In 2015, his wife, Beth, passed into heaven after a three-year battle with stage 4 Cancer. During this time, he felt God was calling him into full-time ministry. A few days after Beth's Celebration of Life service, Wheeler took his two best friends, Brian Roland and Terry Steen, to lunch. He shared his calling with them and they both felt led to join him. Fearless Faith Ministries was born that day.

During the winter of 2016, they began producing daily three-minute inspirational videos on Facebook. They called them, "Your Morning Cup of Inspiration." Today, on Facebook, **Fearless Faith (or FFM 60)** has tens of thousands of followers. Each day viewers are toasted by the guys with their signature mugs featuring their orange three-flame logo.

They have a very popular Instagram page @ **fearlessfaithministries** and a **Fearless Faith** YouTube channel. They can also be reached through their website @ **ffaith.org.**

Followers of Fearless Faith have been requesting a written devotional featuring some of the most popular "Morning Cups of Inspiration." Here it is! These daily inspirations are designed to help you get your day started off with spiritual invigoration. Please begin with the suggested Bible reading followed by "Your Morning Cup of Inspiration." All of the Bible quotes are from the King James Version.

"Our prayer is that these messages will inspire and encourage you to live a fearless life through faith in God. Run your race well and remember to finish strong!"

Dan, Brian and Terry
The Founders of Fearless Faith Ministries

God's Love is Inescapable

Bible Reading: John 3:16; Romans 8:38-39

In 1965, Jackie DeShannon recorded a hit song called, "What the World Needs Now is Love." That song became an anthem for many. The truth is that the world has always needed love. Everybody needs love. It is the most powerful force on earth. How many times have you heard the saying, "Love will conquer all"? That was the name of another hit song recorded in 1986 by Lionel Ritchie.

There is plenty of love to go around. God's love is all around us. Because His very nature is love, He seeks to have a relationship with us. In John 3:16, we read that God loved us so much that He sent His son (Jesus) to die for us. Sin had separated us from God, but He cared so much about us that He allowed His son to die a cruel death on a cross. His love for us allowed Him to look beyond our faults and our sin and pursue us. He pursued us by sending His son to the cross to pay the ultimate price for our sins. We just have to receive the gift of His salvation.

If you are wondering today if anyone loves you, just reach out to God. Ask Jesus to forgive you of your sins and come into your heart. Once you have accepted His love nothing can separate you from it. Death can't and neither can life. Angels can't and neither can demons. The present, the future and any other powers cannot separate you from the love of God. Romans 8:39 tells us that "nothing will be able to separate us from the love of God that is in Christ Jesus our Lord."

You don't need to ever wonder if anyone loves you. The almighty God, the great I Am, the Creator of the Universe loves you more than you can possibly fathom. And because of His love you are more than a conqueror. The world needed love and God sent us His love in the form of His Son.

Ask Yourself: Have I received God's never-ending love into my heart and soul by asking Jesus to forgive me of my sins? Do I realize that God's love has conquered everything, even death, so I don't have to fear tomorrow or any day after that?

Live a Holy Life and Watch God Work

Bible Reading: Joshua 3:5

Maybe you're in a situation where you just don't know what to do. I'm sure you remember the Old Testament story when the children of Israel were told to go possess the promised land and were trying to cross the Jordan River at flood stage. They didn't see a way to cross and didn't know what to do.

The Israelites were looking to Joshua, their God-given leader, hoping he would have the answer. Well, he did have the answer, but it wasn't exactly what they were expecting. He didn't try to overthink it. He didn't have some big strategic plan. He had a very simple approach.

The Bible tells us in Joshua 3:5 that Joshua told the people, "Sanctify yourselves: for tomorrow the Lord will do wonders among you". Sanctify means to set yourself apart for spiritual purposes or purify yourself, be wholly removed of sin. All he asked of the children of Israel was to be holy, not sin, and be ready for what God wanted to do. In essence, just sit back and watch the wonders of God. And a wonder it was, as God parted the waters and the children walked across on dry land.

I don't know you're situation, but sometimes all you need to do is live right before the Lord and sit back and watch. Don't be anxious. Don't be fearful. Sit back in peace, knowing that God is going to do wonders on your behalf. Whatever you're facing, God will take care of it. It's as simple as that. We don't have to make it so complicated. We don't have to try to figure it all out or do it ourselves. We can rely on the Lord. If we do our part, He'll take care of the rest.

Ask God to help you as you commit this day to Him and look forward to the wonders that He's going to perform on your behalf.

Ask Yourself: What do I need to leave in the hands of God today?

Do You Know How Big God Is?

Bible Reading: Psalm 27:3: I Samuel 17:47- 49

Do you know how big and powerful God really is? David did; even as a shepherd boy protecting his flock, he trusted God when he had to fight off lions and bears. When David's brothers were off fighting the Philistines he visited them and took them food. He was shocked to hear the threats being made by a very large member of the Philistine army. Goliath was a giant who made the toughest soldiers in Israel's army tremble with fear. But, David wasn't afraid. In Psalm 27:3 he wrote, "Though an army encamps around me, my heart will not fear; though war breaks out against me, I'll keep my trust." David had complete trust in the Lord, so when Goliath was defying the army of the living God, David took offense and said He would fight the giant. He was confident in God's ability to give him victory.

David actually went into this battle without armor, a spear or even a shield. He took only his slingshot and 5 smooth stones. First Samuel 17:47, tells us that David yelled out to the Philistines, "And all this assembly shall know that the Lord saveth not with sword and spear: for the battle is the Lord's, and he will give you into our hands." Then Goliath started walking down his side of the mountain and into the valley. Instead of retreating or waiting for Goliath, David ran quickly toward him. As he ran he reached into his bag, took out a stone and prepared his sling. He slung it and the stone found its target, striking Goliath on the forehead. The stone sunk deep into his head and he fell face down to the ground. He was dead and David was victorious!

David knew that God was bigger than any problem or any circumstance. But he also came prepared. He prayed often and knew God intimately. He was ready to take on the giant.

Ask Yourself: Am I prepared for life's battles by staying close to God?

Strength from Solitude

Bible Reading: Luke 5:15-16; Matthew 14:22-23

I have a friend who often calls me when he is in the middle of doing something else. When it becomes obvious that he is distracted I say, "It seems like you have something else going on; why don't you call me back when you aren't busy?" He is usually apologetic, but I explain to him that it is frustrating to try and have a conversation with someone who isn't paying attention. Can you imagine what it is like for God when we are attempting to pray but our mind keeps getting distracted by other thoughts? It is important that we schedule our quiet time with the Lord when we can totally focus on Him. I always try to start my day off with Bible reading and prayer. In the morning, I am full of energy and I can focus better before I begin the "busy-ness" of the day.

There are many instances in the Bible when the Lord had to "withdraw from the crowds" so He could focus on God the Father. He usually escaped to the mountains or a desolate place where He could totally focus. The timing of these escapes is also interesting. He usually felt the need to get alone with His heavenly Father right after he had performed a miracle. In the case of today's Bible reading, He had just healed a person with leprosy (Luke 5:15-16) and He had fed five thousand people with five loaves of bread and two fish (Matthew 14: 22-23.) In my life, I have found that when God does something really important the enemy likes to come in and cause me to doubt what happened. Jesus knew that in those times it was important to draw close to God.

Jesus lived a perfect life. He came to earth to show us God in the flesh. He also came to be a shining example of what we should strive to become. We need to follow His practice of spending quiet time with the heavenly Father each and every day. Then, we can gain His strength and His wisdom to face the challenges of a new day.

Ask Yourself: Am I really spending quality time with God every day? Am I able to completely focus my attention on Him?

Bloom Where You're Planted

Bible Reading: I Samuel 16:7

My wife and I wanted some color in our backyard, so we purchased and planted bougainvillea. We went to one nursery and bought a weak, unhealthy and pale plant because the price was right. I planted it in a non-visible, deep corner of the yard, thinking there was no way this thing would make it anyhow.

We went to another nursery and found a beautiful bougainvillea, healthy and deep green. I planted it where it could be seen from the house, and we could enjoy its future beautiful blossoms.

If you visit our backyard today and look at those same two plants, you would be surprised. The beautiful, prominent one is somewhat healthy, but has no blooms. The pale one, planted out of sight, has multiple, beautiful colored blooms and adorns the yard!

Just as I did with those plants, it is easy for us to judge people's potential and value (including ourselves!) by focusing on outward appearances. We think we know whether someone should be in the "prominent corner", where they'll be seen because they're beautiful and surely are going to bloom. Then we put what appears to be the weaker, more anemic one with its issues, over in the far corner where nobody can see it.

Maybe that's you. Maybe you feel like the world has looked at you and put you off into that corner where nobody can see you. They set you there to just exist, not be productive and never bloom.

Remember the story of King David? When Samuel was going to anoint the new king, he looked at all the brothers who were big and strong and said I'm sure it's one of them. It wasn't. It was the little ruddy shepherd boy that was out in the field.

Stop and think about it. You could be the next king. It's not what's on the outside. It's what's on the inside. You and God are the only ones who know whether you're going to bloom or not bloom, whether you're going to grow and be productive where you're planted just like King David.

Ask Yourself: Do I have the mindset to bloom where I'm planted today?

Sinners in the Hands of a Loving God

Bible Reading: I John 3:4; Romans 3:23; Romans 6:23

Sinners in the Hands of an Angry God was a sermon written and preached by British Colonial Christian theologian Jonathan Edwards in 1741. But when I read the Bible, I learn that we are sinners in the hands of a loving God.

The Bible tells us in I John 3:4, "Whosoever committeth sin transgresseth also the law: for sin is the transgression of the law." This verse is referring to the Old Testament law which people had trouble living up to. It also became known as "the law of sin and death." In Romans 3:23 we read, "For all have sinned, and come short of the glory of God." Billy Graham said that, "sin is any thought or action that falls short of God's will. We have all fallen short so we have a sin problem. But Jesus came to earth to fix it."

Another verse in Romans gives us great hope and makes salvation attainable for everyone. Romans 6:23 reads, "For the wages of sin is death; but the gift of God is eternal life through Christ Jesus our Lord." So, by committing sin we have actually earned death because death is the wages of sin. Wages are something we earn. But the verse goes on to say that God gave us a gift. The gift of God is eternal life through Christ Jesus our Lord.

When we sin we earn death but God gave us the gift of eternal life by sending Jesus to die on the cross for our sins. We can't earn or buy our salvation but we can freely accept it. Jesus took our place on the cross. He paid the price for our salvation once and for all. Our salvation is a precious gift from a very loving God. Will you accept it?

Ask Yourself: Have I accepted the gift of eternal life that Jesus Christ earned for me by dying on the cross? Will I show respect for this gift by trying hard every day not to sin?

God Has a Plan for You!

Bible Reading: Jeremiah 29:11; Psalm 46:10; Psalm16:11

Are you at a crossroads? Do you feel like your life is changing directions and you don't know what is around the bend? Remember that God has a plan for your life and His plans include hope and a wonderful future.

As my wife was battling cancer, I felt like God was moving me in a new direction. After she graduated to heaven, I took my two best friends to lunch (Brian and Terry) and I told them that I believed God was calling me into ministry. They both felt the same calling and Fearless Faith Ministries was born. It has been an amazing journey so far and this ministry is growing each day and helping many people along the way. But we didn't know what it would look like on that fall day in 2015 as we talked over lunch.

Maybe you are wondering what God's plan is for you. Ask Him to reveal it to you. Ask Him for wisdom as you seek His new direction. He has only good things planned for you. You may not see your way clearly now, but God will reveal it to you day by day. The most important thing for you to do is to draw near to God. Spend time each day praying for direction and thanking Him for his leading. He has plans to prosper you and not to harm you.

Be still and listen for God's voice. He is about to show you the path of life and fill you with joy as you spend time in His presence. You may not know what the future holds, but you know who holds your future! Walk boldly into it with your hand in the hand of the Creator of the universe! Your future is bright as long as God is at the center of your plans.

Ask Yourself: How can I use my God given talents and abilities in a way that honors God?

Are You a Joyful Person?

Bible Reading: Acts 13:52; Psalm 16:11; John 15:11

Some days I just can't find the joy that I should have as a Christian. To make matters worse, I look around at non-Christians and they seem to be happier than I am. Why do we as Christians struggle with the joy we should have in our lives? I think one reason is the enemy knows that joy is a fruit of the Holy Spirit that we should be producing. So, he attacks us in that very area and tries to place things in our life that would steal or grab away that joy.

It is interesting how the Bible describes the disciples in the book of Acts as they were beginning to grow this brand new church. In Acts 13:52 it says, "And the disciples were filled with joy, and with the Holy Ghost." This is just after they'd been run out of a city. They had joy and the Holy Spirit. So how do you keep that kind of joy in your life? Well, it also says in Psalms 16:11, "...in your presence is fullness of joy,..." You have to get in God's presence and REMAIN there! The only way you can fight off the enemy from trying to steal your joy is to be in the presence of the Lord.

Finally, John talks about the importance of us abiding in the vine, or abiding in Christ. He goes on to tell us if we remain in Him, we'll bear much fruit. Apart from Him we can do nothing. He finishes the chapter by saying, I've told you this so that my joy may be in you and that your joy may be complete. Do you want complete joy in your life as a Christian? Stay in His presence, abide in Him and you can overcome the enemy. You can have the joy in your life that He wants for you and show the fruits of His Spirit as you should.

Ask Yourself: Am I going to walk in joy today?

The Winds Of Life

Bible Reading: Psalm 1:2-4

I love palm trees. Their strength and majesty are beautiful to behold, but when the winds blow, they sway and bend. I've seen their fronds blowing straight out. But palm trees are strong rooted. They rarely break or become uprooted. The Bible compares the spiritual life of a true believer to a tree whose roots run deep. In Psalm 1:2-4, we read, " But his delight is in the law of the Lord; and in his law doth he meditate day and night. And he shall be like a tree planted by the rivers of water, that bringeth forth his fruit in his season; his leaf also shall not wither; and whatsoever he doeth shall prosper. The ungodly are not so: but are like the chaff which the wind driveth away."

Have you experienced winds in your life? Recently, I was staring out my office window on a very windy day and I could see the palm trees swaying in the wind. I noticed how strong and sturdy they were. It was truly an amazing sight because the wind was so great. Many of the old palm fronds had blown off the tree and ended up on the street below, but the tree itself stood firm.

Your life is like a palm tree. The winds of life will sometimes try to uproot you. The old fronds on the palm tree represent problems and troubles you carry with you. The winds may be something caused by you or someone else. Perhaps an area of your life is out of your control. Those winds of life you are feeling may be there to help rid your life of the old palm fronds. On a palm tree, the green beautiful fronds stay put in the heavy winds, but the old fronds that no longer serve a purpose need to blow away. When the winds of life are causing you to worry, try to realize that maybe there are some old problems or relationships that you need to get rid of. Let go and let them blow away trusting that God has something new and something better to take their place.

Ask Yourself: Is their something in my life that is keeping me from experiencing all that God has for me? Is it time for me to let go of them?

Cast Your Cares upon Him

Bible Reading: I Peter 5:7; Matthew 6:25; Philippians 4:6; Proverbs 3:5

Ever since I was a young boy, I heard that I was supposed to cast all my care upon Jesus because He cares for me. I have tried to do that throughout my life, but I've discovered that I have a bad habit of taking them back. I tried to leave them all with Jesus, but I always took them back and continued to worry about them. Do you know anyone who does that? Chances are you are guilty of the same thing.

We all tend to worry about our future, our finances, our relationships, our family and on and on. If we are not careful we can become paralyzed with fear. In I Peter 5:7, the Greek word for "casting" means to throw it on top of Him. Jesus wants us to do this because He is much stronger than we are. We aren't built to carry worry, stress and fear all day long.

In Matthew 6, Jesus basically tells his disciples that they shouldn't worry about anything. He emphasized that every day has enough to worry about so we are to leave tomorrow's problems for tomorrow. Philippians 4:6 tells us, "Be careful for nothing; but in everything by prayer and supplication with thanksgiving let your requests be made known unto God." I think there should be an extra emphasis on the word **NOTHING** in that verse. Jesus basically told His disciples to worry about nothing. There isn't anything in your life that He doesn't know about. He already has it taken care of if you will just believe that He can. God tells us in Proverbs 3:5 that we are to trust in the Lord with all of our heart. And once we cast our cares upon Him we need to leave them in His very capable hands.

Ask Yourself: Do I have enough faith to cast all of my cares on Jesus and never take them back?

The Power of Our Words

Bible Reading: I Samuel 2:35; 3:19

Have you ever walked into a room and there's one person that when they open their mouth and start speaking everybody listens? Then you see another person who could be talking the entire time and it's like he's talking to himself. (I hope that's not you.)

Samuel was an anointed man of God that people listened too. God said He would raise up a faithful priest that would do according to His heart and mind. That was Samuel. Samuel was raised in the temple and had a heart after God.

It's interesting to see the results of somebody that has a heart and mind after God. I Samuel 3:19 reads, "And Samuel grew, and the Lord was with him, and did not let his words fall to the ground." This basically meant that every word Samuel spoke accomplished its purpose.

I remember years ago returning to my alma mater for homecoming and playing in the alumni baseball game. I was playing third base and had a grounder hit to me. I scooped it up to make the throw to first, expecting to hit that first baseman right in the chest. Unfortunately, it hit the ground about 10 feet before it got to first base and eventually rolled to him. I'm sure the runner was safe.

Sometimes that's what happens to our words, isn't it? They fall to the ground short of their target. I didn't have the arm strength anymore. I couldn't get the ball to the first baseman. That can happen with our words as well if they aren't backed by the power and the strength of the Holy Spirit. They don't accomplish their purpose with the needed anointing on our life and on our tongue.

My prayer is that you walk in God's anointing according to His heart and mind. Hopefully, the words you speak will be words that He directs and will have a positive impact causing people to stop and listen. Don't let your words fall to the ground. May they accomplish their intended purpose.

Ask Yourself: Will my words be led by the Holy Spirit today?

You Never Have To Walk In Darkness

Bible Reading: John 8:12; I Peter 2:9; Matthew 5:16

What happens when you walk into a dark room where nothing is visible? The first thing you try to do is get your eyes to adjust to the darkness, and then you feel for a light switch. Once you reach out and flip the switch the room lights up. Without the Lord in your heart your life is like that room. It is full of darkness. Jesus is the source of spiritual light. He wants you to reach out to Him so that He can make the darkness leave your life. He will illuminate your heart and light up your path so you can see your way clearly.

In John 8:12 we read, "Then spake Jesus again unto them, saying, I am the light of the world: he that followeth me shall not walk in darkness, but shall have the light of life." When Jesus says "the light of life", He means you don't have to walk in spiritual darkness. Jesus wants to become the light of your life. When you accept Him as your Lord and Savior, you carry that light within you so you can share it with others. Through your salvation you become a light unto the world.

He will give you a unique message to share with those you come in contact with. You can tell them that they too can have a personal relationship with Jesus. It's not about being religious or living by a set of rules; it's about a relationship with Jesus. Matthew 5:16 reads, "Let your light so shine before men, that they may see your good works, and glorify your Father which is in heaven."

If you haven't done so already, I would encourage you to step out in faith and say this prayer. "Lord, forgive me of my sins. I am a sinner and I ask you to forgive me. I accept you into my life. I want you to be the light in my life so that I never have to live in darkness again. In Jesus name, amen."

Ask Yourself: Is it time for me to step out of the spiritual darkness and let God's glorious light shine in my heart? Am I letting God's light shine for others to see?

God's Perfect Peace

Bible Reading: John 14:27; Philippians 4:7; Isaiah 26:3

Peace is at a premium in today's world. Most people would pay large sums of money to have a peaceful life. There are so many problems, issues and concerns that press in on us every day that peace often seems unimaginable and unachievable. Is it possible to achieve lasting peace in this life?

The Bible tells us that true peace goes beyond our earthly understanding. True peace can be achieved even in the most difficult circumstances. Real peace is not about everything going smoothly. It is about a deep-seated knowledge that everything is going to be okay even when our circumstances seem horribly out of control. Jack E. Dawson illustrated this beautifully in a painting titled, "Peace in the Midst of a Storm." In this painting, he depicts a dark and ominous sky filled with lightning. Rain is pouring down the side of a mountain so hard that water is flowing over the rocks like a raging river. Near the bottom of the painting, however, we see a small bird that is tucked safely inside a hiding place in the cleft of the rock. The bird is seemingly unfazed by the storm.

Jesus is our hiding place. He is our Rock. To know Him is to know true, lasting peace. He told his disciples to not let their hearts be troubled. This life, however, is filled with trouble because we live in a fallen world. However, the Bible tells us in Isaiah 26:3, if we keep our mind stayed on God, He will keep us in perfect peace. This is a lasting peace that goes beyond our earthly understanding.

Ask Yourself: Do you stay focused on God and His peace when your world seems to be falling apart?

How Big Is Your God?

Bible Reading: Psalm 34:3

When I was young I would ask friends, "How do you put an elephant in a milk bottle?" They would reply, "I don't know. How do you put an elephant in a milk bottle?" I went on, "Well, it's really easy. All you have to do is get three things: a milk bottle, a pair of tweezers and binoculars. Then you take the binoculars, turn them backwards and look through them so everything appears very tiny. Focus on the elephant. Now take the tweezers, pick up the elephant by its tail and simply drop it in the milk bottle. How tough is that?" (I'm hoping I was in second grade (not high school) when I told that joke.)

When you look at your God, what end of the binoculars do you look through? I hope you are making him look big today and not tiny. David tells us in Psalms 34:3, "Oh magnify the Lord with me, and let us exalt His name together." My question for you today is are you magnifying your God? Are you making him large?

Remember, this is the same God that formed the universe. This is the God that knows all things, created all things, has always been and forever will be! There is nothing bigger than the God that we serve. Unfortunately, we often make the mistake of shrinking our God down and looking through the binoculars backward. We don't think He has the power to help us do what needs to be done. I want to encourage you to make sure you've got your binoculars facing in the right direction.

Let's magnify the Lord and exalt His name together. We serve a big God. Take full advantage of it.

Ask Yourself: What do I need my BIG God to do for me today?

Am I Enough?

Bible Reading: I Corinthians 1:27

Have you ever wondered how some people have ended up in ministry? Or maybe you see someone who is getting tremendous opportunities and you wonder why, because they don't appear to be extremely gifted or talented. The truth is God can use anyone who makes them selves available to Him.

The Bible tells us in I Corinthians 1:27, "But God hath chosen the foolish things of the world to confound the wise; and God hath chosen the weak things of the world to confound the things which are mighty;" When we look at what is going on today in politics, government, entertainment and industry, we see a lot of foolishness being exposed. God can turn anyone around and He can turn any situation around for His glory.

Maybe as you are reading this, you just can't imagine how God can use you. You might think that you are too ordinary. The Bible is filled with stories of God using ordinary people to accomplish the extraordinary. Maybe you don't think you have any special talents or abilities that God can use. He is more interested in your availability than your ability. Remember, if God calls you to it, He will take you through it.

Are you willing to give God everything you have to accomplish His work today? You might think that you are not enough, but you are as long as you present yourself to Christ as an open vessel and ask Him to use you to be the best you can be for His glory. God will use and multiply whatever you bring to Him.

You may be saying this is not a good time. My attitude is not right. My head is not in the right place. That doesn't matter to God. He wants you to give him all that you are and all that you have right now. Ask God to use you and to open the doors and provide the opportunities for you to serve Him and He will make it happen. Remember, you ARE enough!

Ask Yourself: Am I willing to be used by God in any way He chooses?

The Incredible Power of Prayer

Bible Reading: James 5:14-17; Proverbs 15:8

Have you ever heard someone say, "I guess the only thing we can do is pray?" That statement has always bothered me. It makes it seem like prayer is a last resort when all else has failed. It also minimalizes the power of prayer as if to say, "Well, since we can't do anything else, we might as well pray."

Prayer is everything! James 5:16 reads, "The effectual fervent prayer of a righteous man availeth much." That means that the prayers of a righteous person can cause a lot of good things to happen. We know from James 5:17 that because of the prayers of a man named Elijah, it didn't rain on the earth for three and a half years!!! Prayer changes things!

In the late 1970's, I worked for a Christian television station in Chicago known as TV-38. The founder and president was a man named Owen Carr. Owen was a pastor who believed that Chicago needed a Christian television station so the Gospel message could be brought into the homes of people who would never go to church. He was a man who believed in the power of prayer. He always looked presidential. He was always wearing a nice suit, but if you looked closely you noticed that the knees of his suit pants were always wrinkled. He spent over an hour every morning kneeling in prayer. He almost seemed to glow from being in the presence of Lord. Owen had no television experience yet he was able to pull off the monumental task of bringing a Christian television station to a major city. He believed it happened through the power of prayer.

Prayer is the key to heaven. How can we truly know the Lord if we don't spend time talking to him every day? I like to start praying as soon as I wake up. I know that I need God's presence in my life each and every day. How about you?

Ask Yourself: Am I spending quality time with God every day? Is my prayer time a priority?

Seven Things To Keep
You From Stumbling

Bible Reading: II Peter 1:5-10

We all want to be fruitful and useful in our Christian walk don't we? Peter wrote his second letter from prison. He knew he was about to die and he had some important things to share. One of those things was helping the Church move forward to become more mature in their Christian walk. He wanted them to be more useful and fruitful for the kingdom and not stumble as we so easily tend to do.

Peter listed seven things in that book that we should take some time to reflect on. He said we should diligently increase our faith through: 1. Virtue, meaning moral excellence or our character or our integrity. 2. Knowledge, which would be scriptural understanding or spiritual wisdom, not necessarily intellect. 3. Temperance, or self-control, showing how disciplined we can be. This is so important as we continue to walk and grow in maturity. 4. Patience, or perseverance, reflected by doing the hard things. The hard things are usually the right things. 5. Godliness, or trying our best to live righteously. We must strive to live a life of godliness. The Bible reminds us to be holy for God is holy. Peter finishes up this list with two strong characteristics, 6. Brotherly Kindness, 7. Love.

If you practice moral excellence, knowledge, self-control, perseverance, godliness, kindness and love, something wonderful happens. Peter tells us if we do them, we'll be useful to Him and fruitful in our daily walk!

He concludes this thought by saying if we practice these things we will never stumble. So, if we want to be useful, if we want to be fruitful, if we don't want to stumble, Peter showed us the way. Let's be conscious of these seven things, examine our life, practice them and continue to walk in greater maturity.

Ask Yourself: Will I be diligent in my faith today by practicing these seven things?

Go Boldly Before The Lord

Bible Reading: Hebrews 4:16; Romans 8:16-17

Remember the scene in the Wizard of Oz when Dorothy, the Scarecrow, the Tin Man and the Cowardly Lion go in to see the Wizard to ask for help? They were all frightened out of their minds and could barely speak before the great and powerful Wizard of Oz. When the Wizard yelled at them not to come back unless they brought him the witch's broom, they ran out as fast as they could! God is far more powerful than any wizard and yet the Bible says that we are to go before Him boldly! How can we go before Him boldly?

In Hebrews 4:16 the Bible tells us, "Let us therefore come boldly unto the throne of grace, that we may obtain mercy, and find grace to help in time of need." That doesn't mean to pray like the Pharisees did to impress others. Instead, God wants us to come to Him in the same way that a child would come to his dad to ask for something. In Romans 8:16-17 we read, "The Spirit itself beareth witness with our spirit, that we are the children of God: And if children, then heirs; heirs of

God and joint- heirs with Christ; if so be that we suffer with him, that we may be also glorified together." So we can go boldly before Him because of what Christ did on the cross. We can speak what is on our mind and what is in our heart because we are His children. What happens when a child cries out and asks a parent for help? The parent will do whatever is necessary to comfort that child. God is our heavenly Father and He is going to support you when you ask Him for help. He will guide you and be with you.

Go boldly before the Lord. Speak to Him like you would speak to your parent. He can take whatever you have to tell Him, even if you are angry, upset and frustrated. Tell Him what is bothering you. Tell Him what is good in your life and thank Him for that. But, also, tell Him about what is not so good and ask for His help.

Ask Yourself: Do I speak boldly to God, believing that He loves me as His child?

How Can You Be Truly Happy?

Bible Reading: Matthew 5:3-11

Jesus answered this question in what has come to be known as "The Sermon on the Mount." He laid out eight ways to true happiness. But they are very different from what most of us living in today's world would imagine.

When we think about happiness we usually think about financial success, a beautiful home, a nice car, a loving family and good friends. We might even think about the vacation of a lifetime. But none of these made Jesus' top eight ways to happiness listed in these passages.

The Lord said the "poor in spirit" are blessed or happy. The poor in spirit? They sound depressed. Who are they? Many Bible scholars think Jesus was referring to those who are lowly in their own eyes. They don't exalt themselves but live with humility. Does this sound like you? He went on to say that people who mourn will be happy because they will be comforted. Meek or gentle people are happy according to Jesus because they will inherit the earth. Those who hunger and thirst for righteousness will be filled and, therefore, happy. How are you doing so far? The "pure in heart" will be happy? Jesus said they're happy because they will see God. People who make peace shall be called the children of God and are therefore blessed or happy. I would never put happiness and persecution together but the Lord told us that those who are persecuted for righteousness's sake are happy because they will gain the kingdom of heaven.

Isn't it interesting that Jesus never mentioned money, material possessions or vacations as causing happiness? Instead he listed the opposite. Jesus was referring to eternal happiness. Today let's rethink what makes us happy. Read the beatitudes in Matthew 5. These are the conditions that lead to true, lasting happiness.

Ask Yourself: Am I looking for happiness that will last for just the moment or forever?

Not Feeling Loved Today?

Bible Reading: Romans 5:6-8; 8:35-39

Maybe you're feeling like nobody loves you today. I want to remind you of the deepest relationship you could ever have. You need to hear that God loves you with an everlasting, unconditional love!

There are too many people that say, "How could God possibly love me with everything that I've done, all the times I've sinned, the way I haven't served Him or shown Him any respect or honor?" Romans 5: 6-8 reminds us of the simple truth that Christ died for the ungodly. That's you. That's me.

Paul tells us that somebody *might* die for a righteous or good man. But the ultimate was when Christ demonstrated His own love toward us, by dying for us while we were *still sinners*. That's how much He loves you and me. He died for us. That's the love that He has for us.

Don't lose sight of that today. Don't let the enemy put thoughts into your head that you are not loved or good enough to be loved. God loves you with an undying love.

Paul asks the question in Romans 8:35, "Who shall separate us from the love of Christ? Shall tribulation or distress or persecution or famine or nakedness or peril or the sword?" It continues on.

Then Paul reminds us that we are overcomers through him who loved us. In Romans 8:38-39 he wrote, "For I am persuaded, that neither death, nor life, nor angels, nor principalities, nor powers, nor things present, nor things to come, nor height, nor depth, nor any other creature, shall be to separate us from the love of God which is in Christ Jesus our Lord."

There's not a thing you can do to change or reduce the amount of love God has for you. Never forget that YOU ARE LOVED!

Ask Yourself: How can I thank God for for His incredible love today?

How Far is Heaven?

Bible Reading: Genesis 1:1; John 14:2; John 3:16; 2 Corinthians 5:1

In 2004, Los Lonely Boys recorded a song entitled, *Heaven.* The first line of the song says, "I know there's a better place than this place I'm living. How far is heaven?" Well, no human being knows the answer to that question, but according to the Bible, heaven is a very real place.

Heaven is mentioned 622 times in the Bible. The very first verse of the Bible, Genesis 1:1 says, "In the beginning God created the heaven and the earth." Jesus mentioned heaven 70 times in the New Testament. He also referred to it in John 14:2, where he says, "In my Father's house are many mansions: if it were not so, I would have told you. I go to prepare a place for you."

A great book on the subject is *Imagine Heaven* by John Burke. In this fascinating book, Burke shares over one hundred stories of people who were clinically dead or near death, and revived to share amazing details of their experiences.

These were orthopedic surgeons, airline pilots, professors and neurosurgeons. They were basically people who had very little to gain and everything to lose if they were making things up. They were different ages, backgrounds and faiths. Yet, they all painted a similar, grand picture of heaven.

Recently, we were doing "man on the street" interviews and we asked several people if they believed in an afterlife. There were some amusing answers, some really thoughtful and others that were flippant about it. Most were not sure if there was a heaven, but if it was a real place, they all hoped to go there one day.

The Bible not only tells us of the place but also describes it to us. If you believe the Bible is the inspired Word of God then you can trust that heaven is a real place. In II Corinthians 5:1 we read, "For we know that if the earthly house of this tabernacle were dissolved, we have a building of God, an house not made with hands, eternal in the heavens." Heaven may be closer than you think.

Ask Yourself: Do I live my life in anticipation of going to heaven one day?

To Be A Sheep

Bible Reading: John 10:27-28; Proverbs 3:5-6

Most of us desire to be strong, independent and brave. It sounds like the description of a lion doesn't it? However, in the Bible, God often compares us to sheep. Why would anyone want to be compared to sheep?

Sheep are not independent; instead, they are entirely dependent on their shepherd. Their shepherd feeds and protects them. God does the same for us. Sheep know their shepherd's voice and follow him. They like to stay close to him. We need to follow God's voice and His leading. Like sheep, we feel safe in the presence of our Good Shepherd.

Although it is easy to follow other people we need to stay close enough to the Lord so that we know His voice and we follow His leading. Are you close enough to the Lord that you know His voice and can distinguish it from the thousands of other voices that you hear every day? I saw a video once of a Shepherd calling his sheep. The entire flock responded immediately and ran very quickly toward their shepherd when they heard his voice. Other sheepherders tried calling his flock using the same words. They even tried to mimic his voice. The sheep weren't fooled. They knew their shepherd's voice so well that they never followed a pretender.

As the passage in John chapter 10:27 tells us that God's sheep know His voice and follow Him. When we trust in Him with all our heart, and acknowledge Him in all our ways He directs our paths. He wants to give us wisdom in all of our decisions. The key is listening and following. He will never lead you where His grace cannot keep you.

Ask Yourself: Am I spending enough time reading God's Word, praying and listening? Am I seeking God's direction in every area of my life?

Help Somebody In Need Today

Bible Reading: James 1:27; Luke 14:13-14

I was in a large home improvement store the other night to purchase something I needed. I looked down a side aisle and noticed a lady riding a mobile cart and realized she wasn't able to get around very well. I saw her looking up at the wall of tools and recognized her dilemma. I quickly went around a couple aisles to get in front of her and asked if she needed help.

I proceeded to pull down the different tool options and helped her look them over without getting up. She decided on one, put it in her basket and then said, "Let me get out of your way so you can get in here and get what you were looking for." I replied, "I'll be honest. I wasn't looking for anything here. I just came over to help you." She was so moved and touched by that and seemed very appreciative. It was such a simple thing, but it made me realize how important simple things can be.

In James 1:27, we learn that the purest form of religion before God is when we help people like orphans and widows, who cannot help themselves. It reinforces to us the importance of helping the needy, doing something for somebody who can't do something in return.

Luke 14:13 re-emphasizes this by telling us when you give a feast invite the poor, the maimed, the lame, the blind and you'll be blessed because they can't repay you. However, it finishes by saying we will be repaid at the resurrection.

I encourage you to go out today and keep your eyes open for somebody to help. That's pure religion and pleases God. Your reward might be a big smile or you might not receive anything until you reach eternity. Help somebody in need today!

Ask Yourself: Who can I help that cannot return the favor?

Are You Called?

Bible Reading: John 6:44; Matthew 5:16

Have you ever heard anyone say that they were called into the ministry? What does that really mean? Can anyone be called to do the Lord's work?

If you've been in Christian circles or grew up in the church, you may have heard someone say they had a calling on their life to go into the ministry. Some people say they were called to be priests as kids growing up in Catholic school. Being "called" does not only pertain to becoming a minister, priest or missionary. We are all called by Christ to accept Him as our authority and to have a personal relationship with Him. In John 6:44, the Bible tells us that when Jesus was talking to the crowd He said, "No man can come to me, except the Father which hath sent me draw him: and I will raise him up at the last day."

Christ draws all of us to Him by putting the desire to know Him in our heart. It's up to us to make the decision to follow and accept the Lord as our Savior or not. Jesus gives us the freewill to accept or reject Him. But, we are all called because Christ came to earth to reconcile us with God the father.

When Adam and Eve disobeyed God in the Garden of Eden, they created a chasm between man and God. Through the death and resurrection of Jesus Christ, you can now have direct communion with God the Father. God has called all of us to draw near to Him and have a personal relationship with Him.

After we accept Christ as Lord of our life there is work to be done. You are called to serve in God's kingdom. God may call you into full- time ministry or He may have a ministry for you to the people you come in contact with every day at work or social activities. God tells us in Matthew 5:16, "Let your light so shine before men, that they may see your good works, and glorify your Father which is in heaven." You have a calling to do good works and to let your light shine to all who come in contact with you every day.

Ask Yourself: Am I living my "calling" each and every day?

What Can You Expect from God?

Bible Reading: Joshua 1:5; Psalm 16:11

Have you ever been let down by a friend or a close family member? Maybe you were expecting them to help you with a project and they never showed up. Perhaps you made plans to spend the day together and, at the last minute, they called and canceled. Or, worse yet, maybe they said something hurtful about you behind your back. All of us, at some point, have been disappointed and hurt by the words or actions of someone close to us.

If you are a Christian you can trust that God will never let you down. In Joshua 1:5, He promises that He will never fail you or forsake you. What an amazing promise. God is not like humans. His Word is true and faithful. We can count on every one of His promises. He is the one friend who will never disappoint!

God wants the very best for you and me. All we have to do is ask Him for it. He knows what path we should take when we are lost. He wants to give us knowledge and wisdom.

Psalm 16:11 reads, "Thou wilt shew me the path of life: in thy presence is fullness of joy; at thy right hand there are pleasures for evermore." That is an exciting promise! The Creator of all life wants to show you and me the right path to follow to live a fulfilling life. And the best part is we don't have to walk it alone. He will walk beside us as we follow His path. In the same verse, we read that God will fill us with joy in His presence and with eternal pleasures. We can expect God to always be with us. These promises are not just for this life. This verse goes on to say that He will give us pleasures forevermore. Does it get any better than that? He promised us all these things now and forever. We can count on Him! We can expect great things from our Great God and we will not be disappointed.

Ask Yourself: Am I better off making decisions based on my own wisdom or God's? Am I truly seeking His wisdom in all that I say and do every day of my life?

Do ALL Things Without Grumbling!

Bible Reading: Philippians 2:14-15

You've probably heard the story about the wife trying to get her husband out of bed on Sunday morning to go to church. He rolled over saying, "I don't want to go today! The sermons could always be better. I just think we could find a better church and I'm just tired. I don't feel like going!" At which the wife replied, "Honey, we go through this every Sunday. You have to go. You're the pastor!"

Maybe you feel like that some mornings. You just don't want to get up and do what you've got to do. I had one of those mornings yesterday. Everything that could go wrong in my job seemed to go wrong. I had deals starting to fall through and things that I thought were completed were not. There were complications and one thing after another started piling up. I was getting frustrated and annoyed and began grumbling. I went to bed that night hoping in the morning things would be better. But when I woke up in the morning,

I was like that pastor. I did not want to go to work and the first thing I did was begin grumbling.

Then I realized what God's Word says about grumbling. In Philippians 2:14-15, "Do all things without murmurings and disputings: that ye may be blameless and harmless, the sons of God, without rebuke, in the midst of a crooked and perverse nation, among whom ye shine as lights in the world." Wow! If we grumble like the world grumbles, we're no different than the world.

You may need to step up your game. You are not to grumble. You are to be different. That's how people will see your light. If your office atmosphere is full of grumbling, but people notice that you don't grumble, there's your light shining! That's your challenge today. Let's go through the day without grumbling.

Ask Yourself: Can I make it through the day without grumbling?

Are You Living with Passion?

Bible Reading: Ecclesiastes 9:10; Colossians 3:23

Have you ever been around someone who is really passionate about what they do? Their passion tends to become contagious and it affects everyone around them. You can tell that they honestly love their work. People who are passionate about their work don't look at it as a job they look at it as their calling.

As Christians, we all have a calling. Once you accept the Lord as your Savior and you realize that you have the great hope of eternal life in heaven, you want to tell other people about your experience. Your focus is less on you and more on Jesus as you allow Him to shine through your life.

King Solomon was perceived to be the wisest person who ever lived. He tells us in Ecclesiastes 9:10, "Whatsoever thy hand findeth to do, do it with thy might...." So, whatever your job is, your real calling is to reach others with God's love. Part of that calling is to be passionate about everything you do including your job.

While you probably have a boss at work, your ultimate boss is God. You need to realize that He is always watching to see if you are doing your very best. Colossians 3:23 says, "And whatsoever ye do, do it heartily, as to the Lord, and not unto men." You can easily change the word "heartily" to "passionately."

Do you tend to act a little differently when your boss comes around? Perhaps you pick up your energy a bit or you try to look like you are working really hard on something. Remember, your real boss is always watching and He is hoping you will make Him proud.

Ask Yourself: Am I living my life with passion? Am I working to please God or others?

Just Show Up!

Bible Reading: II Corinthians 12:9; Philippians 3:13-14

When my wife was diagnosed with stage 4 cancer, many people called and told me that if I needed anything to just ask. I never asked. I was so busy taking care of her that I didn't have time to even think about asking someone for help. If you have a friend or family member who is going through a rough time don't say that to them. Instead, just show up and be there for them. They are so focused on their problem that they don't have time to call and ask for your help. Don't worry about what you will say. Just give them a hug and be present with them. They need you to be a friend! Go to their house, hug them, listen to them, bring them food and help them in any way you can.

Several friends showed up for me during my darkest hours and I will never forget that they did. Several brought food over and physically put it in my refrigerator during Beth's final days. I had a house full of people but I was too busy caring for my wife to think about food. Another friend came to visit and brought a box of soft pretzels for everyone to snack on.

Jesus never promised us an easy life. However, He did say that His grace is sufficient for us and that His strength is made perfect in weakness. We are not always strong and we don't always feel good. But we have to show up every day and rely on His strength to pull us through when we are weak. We also need friends who will come along beside us. So give the gift of your presence to someone who is facing difficult circumstances. Don't worry about what you will say to them. They probably won't remember anything that you say but they will remember how you make them feel.

Ask Yourself: Do I know someone who is going through a hard time who could use a visit from me?

The Highs and Lows of Life

Bible Reading: I Kings Chapters 18-19

Let's face it. You can't be on a high every day. You're going to have your high days and low days. If you're having a high day, good for you. But, maybe you're not. Maybe you're down today. Maybe it was a doctor's phone call. Maybe it was your boss saying something that brought you down. Things can bring you down, but you don't have to stay there.

Even Elijah, one of the greatest prophets in the Bible, couldn't be "up" every day. The 18th and 19th chapter of I Kings tells the story of the ups and downs of Elijah's life. He had challenged four hundred and fifty prophets of Baal to have their god send fire down from heaven and consume their sacrifices. But, they couldn't do it.

When it was Elijah's turn, he told them to pour water over his sacrifice and then simply asked God to provide the fire, which He did in an amazing way. Elijah was on a high. Unfortunately, the king's wife, Jezebel, found out what happened and was determined to kill Elijah. So what did this great prophet of God do? He ran away and hid and lost all of his self-confidence.

Does that sound like you on a bad day? The good news is you don't have to stay there. Elijah finally went to God and God helped him. If you're down today, you can go to God and He'll do the same thing for you.

First, God will encourage you. Elijah thought he was the only prophet of God left but God reassured him there were over 7,000 still alive that he was unaware of. This brought Elijah comfort.

Second, God will give you a new assignment, giving you fresh purpose for this life. That's what God did for Elijah. So if you're down today, go to the Lord and ask him to encourage you. Ask him to help you refocus on the new day.

Ask Yourself: What fresh purpose does God have for me to focus on today?

How Do You React to People in Conflict?

Bible Reading: II Timothy 3:1-5; Luke 12:53; I Peter 3:8-9; I John 3:18

Many people are deeply conflicted today. They are conflicted on politics, morality and priorities. Read what Paul said to Timothy in II Timothy 3:1-5, "This know also, that in the last days perilous times shall come. For men shall be lovers of their own selves, covetous, boasters, proud, blasphemers, disobedient to parents, unthankful, unholy, without natural affection, trucebreakers, false accusers, incontinent, fierce, despisers of those that are good, traitors, heady, high-minded, lovers of pleasures more than lovers of God; Having a form of godliness, but denying the power thereof: from such turn away." Does that sound like people today?

Luke 12:53, goes on to say, "The father shall be divided against the son, and the son against the father; the mother against the daughter, and the daughter against the mother; the mother in law against her daughter in law, and the daughter in law against her mother in law."

The Bible clearly tells us what people will be like in end times and it sounds very similar to the world we are living in right now. Many have turned away from any kind of faith in God. Instead, they are putting their faith in themselves. So how are we to react to them? I Peter 3:8-9 tells us, "Finally, be ye all of one mind, having compassion one of another, love as brethren, be pitiful, be courteous: Not rendering evil for evil, or railing for railing: but contrariwise blessing; knowing that ye are thereunto called, that ye should inherit a blessing."

How will you approach your day today knowing that you're probably going to run into someone that disagrees with everything you think and believe? First John 3:18 says, "My little children, let us not love in word, neither in tongue; but in deed and in truth." Let love show in your actions today.

Ask Yourself: Am I reacting in love to those whose beliefs are very different from mine?

God's Perfect Timing

Bible Reading: 2 Corinthians 5:7; Genesis 12:1-3; Romans 9:9; Ecclesiastes 3:1-8

Are you tired of waiting? Have you been praying for an answer to a problem and you feel like God is just refusing to answer? Are you growing discouraged because the answer doesn't seem to be coming any time soon? If you answered yes to any of these questions you are normal. We all want answers to our prayers and we want them NOW!!!

God hears your prayers. The answer is on its way. But it will come in God's time not yours. God's time is not just "in time" "convenient" or "good." God's timing is PERFECT! I had certain goals and dreams that I had let go of because I thought they would never happen. In God's perfect timing, however, they did! It was usually way past the time that I thought they should have happened, but the timing ended up being better than I ever thought possible!

The Bible is filled with stories about timing but I will just remind you of one of the most important. God promised

Abraham that He would make a mighty nation from Abraham's seed. Abraham waited patiently for 15 years, but he and Sarah remained childless well into their old age. God visited him again and reassured him that the promise was coming, but it took another 10 years for it to actually come true. Finally, it did when Abraham and Sarah gave birth to a son named Isaac. Abraham was 100 and Sarah was 91! It was a BIG promise. It took a long time, but God delivered on His promise.

In Ecclesiastes 3:1-8, we read that there is a season and a time to every purpose under the heaven. This means God will bring about His ultimate purpose for your life in His perfect timing. His answer is coming. Look for it!

Ask Yourself: Do I really believe that God will accomplish His perfect will in my life in His perfect time? Am I willing to wait for it?

A New Heaven and a New Earth

Bible Reading: Revelation 21-22; James 5:7-8

I did it! I finished the Bible one more time. What a great ending. The last two chapters of Revelation give us hope. As Christians, there's no better hope than Revelation teaching that Jesus is coming back to take us to heaven to live with him for eternity. I wonder about people who do not have that eternal hope. How do you really live life joyfully and in peace without the belief that there's more than we're living for right now?

Be aware that if you haven't received Christ as your Savior then that hope is not available to you. So I encourage you to believe in Him today. Accept Him as your Savior and Lord. Once you do, that promise is available to you as well.

The Bible says there's going to be a new heaven and a new earth and we're going to reign for eternity in God's presence. We're going to literally be living with God! That is something worth having the faith to believe and hope for. I pray that you do.

The Bible also tells us that a day is like a thousand years in eternity. So, the good works we do today, the temporary things, are important because they're actually storing up treasures in heaven. The way we live now is going to determine how well we live in eternity.

James 5:7-8 says, "Be patient therefore, brethren, unto the coming of the Lord. Behold, the husbandman waiteth for the precious fruit of the earth, and hath long patience for it, until he received the early and latter rain. Be ye also patient; stablish your hearts for the coming of the Lord draweth nigh."

Be patient. Establish your heart. Allow your faith to grab hold of that hope of Christ's return and that you will spend eternity with Him.

Ask Yourself: How can I live today with an eye on eternity?

Who Are You Trying To Impress?

Bible Reading: Romans 12:3-4

God made only one **you.** Nobody else has your fingerprint or your DNA. When he formed you in your mother's womb, He made you unique. He gave you special gifts and abilities that nobody else has. He wants you to use those gifts to help other people and to glorify Him. He doesn't want you to try to act like someone else simply to impress others.

Many people take pride in who they are and what they have. However, God wants you to remain humble and grateful for what He has given you. We all have a place on God's team. Romans 12:3-4 reads, "For I say, through the grace given unto me, to every man that is among you, not to think of himself more highly than he ought to think; but to think soberly, according as God hath dealt to every man the measure of faith. For as we have many members in one body, and all members have not the same office: so we, being many are one body in Christ, and everyone members one of another."

You were created to honor and glorify God in all that you

do. In Colossians 3:23 we read, "And whatsoever ye do, do it heartily, as to the Lord, and not unto men; Knowing that of the Lord ye shall receive the reward of inheritance; for ye serve the Lord Christ." Your mission is not to impress other people.

Jesus always spoke the truth and the religious leaders of His time were often offended. He didn't do things the way they thought He should. But Jesus never let their opinions change His mission. He came to speak the truth because that is what His heavenly Father sent Him to do. The only one that He wanted to please was His heavenly Father. In the same way, we should worry about pleasing God not man.

Run your own race. Do the job that you have been called to do and be faithful to use the gifts God has given you.

Ask Yourself: Am I doing things to please God or others?

Martha's Dilemma

Bible Reading: Luke 10:38-42; Psalms 37:7; Psalms 46:10

Are you all tangled up in knots worrying about your problems? Do you feel like you always have so much to do that there aren't enough hours in the day to get it all done? Do you feel like you can't find time to be alone with God because of your never ending "To Do List?"

There is a story in the Bible about a woman who wrestled with the same problems. Her name was Martha. We read in Luke 10:38 that Martha received Jesus into her house. Now that would be a pretty big deal. As you can imagine, Martha wanted everything to be just perfect. In verse 39 we read about Martha's sister, Mary. She just sat at Jesus' feet to hear Him speak while Martha was busy serving Jesus. This really bothered Martha. She felt like she was doing all the work while Mary was just sitting around. In verse 40 it says, "But Martha was cumbered about much serving." The word cumbered means hampered or hindered. So while Mary was just enjoying being in the presence of the Lord, Martha couldn't enjoy anything because she was hampered by all of her busy-ness. She went to Jesus and complained about her sister. Jesus' answer surprised her. In Luke 10:41 Jesus said, "Martha, Martha, thou art careful and troubled about many things: But one thing is needful: and Mary hath chosen that good part, which shall not be taken away from her." Wow! Jesus told Martha that her priorities were in the wrong place.

Can you relate to Martha? Do you have trouble trying to relax in the presence of the Lord? Jesus wants you to take a break from your troubles and your worries. He wants you to spend time just renewing yourself in His presence. Today He wants you to be still and know that He is God!

Ask Yourself: When was the last time that I really took a break from my worries and just focused on being in God's presence?

Really God? That's the Best You Could Do?

Bible Reading: Zephaniah 3:5

How many times have you said to God, "Really God, that's the best you could do? You REALLY messed up this time! I thought for sure you'd have seen that coming." I've reacted like this way too many times and I'm sure you have as well.

How many times have you been in a situation where you pray something would go a certain way and God "let's you down". Maybe you're there today. Maybe there is something going on in your life right now and you're saying, "You could see this ahead of time God, why didn't you stop it? Why did you allow this to happen to my family and me?" I'm sure if you stopped and thought, you could think of a time or circumstance you felt God had let you down.

The following verse may help you refocus on the bigger picture and see things from a different perspective. Zephaniah 3:5 says, "every morning doth he bring his judgment to light, he faileth not; but the unjust knoweth no shame." That's right! You may think otherwise, but God never fails. He's always right. He's always righteous, never unrighteous. He's never too early. He's never too late. He's always on time.

Whatever you're going through, remember God never fails. If you are following God to the best of your ability, trying to hear His voice, being obedient and trusting Him, you can be confident that He has your best in mind.

He has a purpose for what you're going through. He'll not let you down. He's not forsaken you. He's not walked away from you. He's not condemned you. So refocus your thoughts away from the situation and thoughts that God failed you. Instead, focus on the purpose and reason that God has you in this situation. God never fails and is always working out things for your good!

Ask Yourself: Do I believe that through ALL circumstances God will never fail me?

Why Did Jesus Come To Earth?

Bible Reading: Isaiah 9:6

Why did Jesus come to earth? Why was he born? Why did God send him in the form of a baby? He came to make things right. When Adam and Eve sinned in the Garden everything was broken. The relationship between God and man was broken so God sent His son Jesus to make everything right again.

If you listen to the news, it is obvious that we live in a broken world. People have turned away from God and are overflowing with frustration. They're angry and they lash out because they feel that no one is listening to them. But Christ came to this world in the form of a baby to prove His love for us. It wasn't just his birth; it continued through his death and resurrection. When He arose from the dead, He set the stage to finalize His mission to make things right. Through His resurrection, He gave us direct communion with God, just as Adam and Eve enjoyed in the Garden of Eden. His resurrection gave us new life and a guarantee of eternity.

Because Christ overcame death, we can live in God's glory forever. When we simply accept Jesus as the Lord of our life, we are in perfect communion with Him and can go to Him boldly with our requests. God sent His son, Jesus Christ, to make things right. In Isaiah 9:6, the Bible tells us "For unto us a child is born, unto us a son is given: and the government shall be upon his shoulder: and his name shall be called Wonderful, Counselor, The mighty God, The everlasting Father, The Prince of Peace."

Look at the government today and what do you see? Everybody is right and no one is wrong. All you see is a tangled mess. I love the line in Isaiah 9:6 that says, "And the government shall be upon his shoulder." Jesus is the ultimate authority and as the government, He will make things right.

Ask Yourself: Have I asked Jesus to make things right in my life?

Let Go and Let God!

Bible Reading: Matthew 11:28-29; II Corinthians 12:9

The game of golf mirrors the game of life. In golf the harder you try the worse you do. If you try to squeeze the club too hard your swing isn't smooth and the ball doesn't respond well at contact. If you swing too hard the ball usually ends up going in the wrong direction. The key to a great golf swing is to loosen your grip on the club and make a smooth swing. The same is true in life.

Are you in a situation where you are trying to force your own way and it just isn't working? Maybe you are in a relationship and you are trying hard to make the other person think and act a certain way, and they just aren't responding in the way that you want. Perhaps you are in a situation at work where you are trying extremely hard, but it seems like your efforts go "unnoticed." The harder you try the more frustrated you become. Maybe you have a child who doesn't want to do things your way anymore and you feel like you are fighting with everything you have to hold on to them.

The Bible tells us that it doesn't have to be so hard. In Matthew 11:28, Jesus says to come unto to Him and He will give us rest. In fact, He tells us that we will find rest for our souls. In II Corinthians 12:9, we learn that God's strength is made perfect in our weakness.

The fact is that we often try too hard. What God really wants us to do is to trust Him with every situation. He wants us to pray about every situation and then leave it in His hands. He wants to know if we trust Him enough to let go of our situation or problem and give it to Him. Maybe it is time to let go and let God!

Ask Yourself: Do I trust God enough to let go and let God take over each and every situation in my life?

What Are You Waiting For?

Bible Reading: Acts 22:13-16

In Acts 22, Paul was sharing his testimony and defending himself before a crowd. He was sharing what took place during the Damascus Road experience when he was blinded and God stopped him in his tracks. God sent Ananias, a good Christian in the area, to go speak to him. In Acts 22:13, Ananias told Paul (then Saul) to receive his sight. As soon as he said it, Paul was able to see again. How miraculous was that? And then he said in verse 14, "The God of our fathers has chosen thee, that thou shouldest know his will."

Just like Paul, God has chosen you! You and I are no different than Paul. We can instantaneously have our spiritual eyes opened, and know that He has chosen us. He has chosen you to do His will today. Then in Acts 22:15, "For thou shalt be His witness unto all men of what thou hast seen and heard." Paul's marching orders are the same marching orders for you and me today.

We are to be a witness of what we've seen and heard. It's as simple as that. It's basically what we refer to as our testimony. The story of what we've gone through in life and what we've learned. It is what God has put on your heart to share with someone else, the things that you've seen and heard.

Encourage those you come in contact with today by sharing your testimony, your life stories, letting them know what God has done for you. It may renew their spirits and give them the wisdom that they need.

Ananias asked Paul in the sixteenth verse of Acts chapter 22, he said, "And now why tarriest thou? Arise, and be baptized, and wash away thy sins, calling on the name of the Lord." So my question for you today is, "Why are you waiting?" There's no reason to wait. I pray you have a "spiritual eye opening" experience today. Know that you've been chosen by God. Share your testimony. There is no need to wait any longer.

Ask Yourself: Who can I share my testimony with today?

Do You Have A Saul In Your Life?

Bible Reading: I Samuel 18:6-16; I Samuel 24:3-4

Do you have something or someone in your life that is holding you back? Is someone using you to get ahead or talking behind your back? Has someone literally become a thorn in your side?

David had that kind of person in his life. His name was King Saul. He became so jealous of David's success that he wanted to kill him. When David was trying to soothe the King's tormented spirit by playing the harp, Saul picked up a spear and threw it at him. Even though Saul made several attempts on his life, David continued to faithfully serve him.

David had a chance to kill Saul when the king entered a cave where David and his men were hiding. In 1 Samuel 24:3-4, David had a chance to kill King Saul but he refused to harm him because Saul was God's chosen leader. At the same time, David believed that God was using these events to teach him, and to help him reach his destiny.

How do you react when someone is throwing spears at

you? Maybe they are throwing spears of hatred, lies and deceit. What do you do when someone is smearing your name to co-workers, family or friends? These are the "Sauls" in your life and how you react to them determines your spiritual growth. Do you react to them the same way they are acting towards you, or do you remain gracious and kind, knowing that God is using them to mature you? You can't do it alone. You need an ally. You need someone to constantly work behind the scenes for you. That someone is Jesus. Ask Him to help you face the "Sauls" in your life. He will honor your prayers and help you grow in your faith whenever you face adversity in your spiritual walk with Him.

Ask Yourself: Do I react in kindness and love toward those who try to hurt me?

How Great Thou Art

Bible Reading: Psalm 89:5-8

There have been many great recordings of the song *How Great Thou Art* through the years. Elvis recorded a powerful rendition of it on an album by the same title in 1966. In fact, that album won Elvis a Grammy award for Best Sacred Performance. Carrie Underwood and Vince Gill knocked it out of the park with their performance of the song at the American Country Music's Girls Night Out in 2011.

Sadly, the writer of this amazing song never knew the impact of his words. Carl Boberg, a Swedish pastor wrote the lyrics as a poem in 1885 titled, *O Great God.* He was inspired to pen the words when he heard church bells in the midst of a terrible thunderstorm. It wasn't until several years later that the words were set to a Swedish folk tune. Boberg passed away in 1940 long before the song caught on in America. Stuart K. Hine first translated the song into English in 1949 and George Beverly Shea made it popular by singing it at Billy Graham crusades in 1954.

Today millions of people around the world continue to sing this beautiful song that gives God all praise and glory as the Creator of the Universe. It so poignantly portrays God's power and beauty as seen in creation. I particularly love the words to the chorus. "Then sings my soul, My Savior God to Thee, How Great Thou art, How Great Thou Art."

Maybe you shared your faith with someone and you wondered if they listened to anything you said. Perhaps you served as an usher or a greeter in church and you wondered if your smile and cheerful demeanor had an impact on anyone. Carl Boberg is an example of how God can use our work in a powerful way long after our time on earth is finished.

Ask Yourself: Have you ever done something as a form of service to God that only God knew about?

Never Take a Day For Granted

Bible Reading: Psalm 34:1; Philippians 4:13

I was recently enjoying a fun Sunday afternoon stroll with my wife along one of our beautiful causeways here in Florida. Walking along the side of the bay, enjoying the artistry of God's nature, I just had to stop and take it all in. At that moment, I realized how much God had blessed my wife and me with the life He has given us. I made a mental note that I should never take another day for granted.

Beyond the beauty, I realized that I was walking along with no pain in my body. Hey, at this age, that's a victory in itself! You never want to lose sight of those things. As long as you have breath in your lungs, there will be reason to be thankful and grateful for each day.

I want to encourage you, wherever you are, whatever you're going through, find something to praise the Lord for. You need to approach your day like David when he said in Psalm 34:1, "I will bless the Lord at all times: his praise shall continually be in my mouth." I encourage you to do that. Find something to praise the Lord for, because it's there.

It's possible you may be going through a trial or valley right now. Maybe you're going through something so deep you don't think you can find it in you to be grateful. You don't think you can dig down that deep to find something to praise the Lord for. All I can say is, "try"! I think with God's help you'll find you can. Paul reminds us in Philippians 4:13, that we can do all things through Christ who strengthens us and He'll give you strength for the day. Whatever it is you're going through, He'll help you through.

So get out there and be grateful, never taking another day for granted.

Ask Yourself: What can I be grateful for today?

Show Kindness to All

Bible Reading: Colossians 3:12; Luke 6:35; Romans 12:14

In this day and age it seems like everyone is right and nobody is wrong. As Christians, we seem to be targets for those who are mad at God. Many blame Him for their lives not turning out the way they expected so they take it out on Christians. They often resent the peace that true Christians have in their lives. We need to be very careful to always show these people kindness. We need to be Christ-like and treat everyone with pure love and kindness.

But how do we do that? To be like Jesus is to show genuine, undeserved kindness to others. The Bible tells us in Colossians 3:12, "Put on therefore, as the elect of God, holy and beloved, bowels of mercies, kindness, humbleness of mind, meekness, longsuffering;" These five emotions are characteristics of God.

The Bible also tells us to love our enemies. Wait. What? How in the world do we love our enemies when they are constantly attacking us? In Luke 6:35, the Bible says, " But love ye your enemies, and do good, and lend, hoping for nothing again; and your reward shall be great, and ye shall be the children of the Highest: for he is kind unto the unthankful and to the evil."

But what do we do when someone mistreats us? Well, let's think about how Jesus would react. If you go to Romans 12:14 in the New Testament of your Bible you will read, "Bless them which persecute you: bless, and curse not." This is easier said than done and this is why we need to ask Jesus to help us in all matters. He won't ever let you down. He will guide you through the landmines of life so that you will become a "beacon of light" in a world of darkness that desperately needs the love and kindness of Christ.

Ask Yourself: Do I consistently show the kindness of Christ to others?

Leave a HUGE Inheritance

Bible Reading: Proverbs 31:25-31; Ecclesiastes 9:10

What kind of an inheritance do you want to leave your children and grandchildren? Most of us would love to leave something for our loved ones whether it be in the form of money, property or a vehicle. But the best type of an inheritance doesn't involve money or things. It's a spiritual legacy.

My earliest memories include church. My mom made sure that all of her children learned about Jesus from an early age. She made sure that we were in church on Sunday morning, Sunday evening and Wednesday evening. There were no excuses. But more importantly, she taught us how to pray and read our Bible. I remember having prayer time with her and she made us kneel when we prayed in reverence to our almighty Creator. She taught us that we needed to ask Jesus to forgive us of our sins and invite Him into our heart.

Finally, we saw the way that she lived out her Christianity. She was loving, honest and giving. She was one of the hardest workers that I ever knew. I learned that hard work was not only Important to be successful, but that as a Christian, I needed to always give my best. My mom believed that Christians should always strive to be the best. Ecclesiastes 9:10 says, "Whatsoever thy hand findeth to do, do it with thy might." My mom made sure that we understood what that meant. She loved the Lord with all her heart. She tithed to the church faithfully and was always willing to help others in need.

My mom passed into heaven on May 7, 2018 at the age of ninety-six. She certainly lived up to Solomon's description of a woman of noble character in the thirty-first chapter of Proverbs. She didn't leave us any money but she left an inheritance worth far more than all the riches on earth.

Ask Yourself: What kind of an inheritance or legacy will I leave my loved ones when my time on earth is finished?

Controlling Our Tongue

Bible Reading: James 3:1-7; Proverbs 11:12-14

The Bible tells us in James that to be able to control the tongue we have to be perfect. James goes on to describe our tongue as a bit in a horse's mouth, the rudder of a ship and tongues of fire. All of these examples show how it controls something much larger than itself. No wonder the tongue so easily controls us as well.

Unfortunately, if you have not developed your faith and deepened your relationship with the Holy Spirit, you will not be able to control your tongue the way God wants you to. It's the Holy Spirit that gives you the self-control you need. I encourage you to seek to deepen your faith that God would naturally help you control your tongue and say the things that He wants you to say. And more importantly, He'll help you not say the things that displease Him.

Additionally, Proverbs 11:12-14 reminds us of three different things regarding our tongue. First, it says a man of understanding holds his peace. You have to know when to hold your tongue and not get yourself in trouble or hurt people.

Second, it says a faithful spirit conceals a matter. You are not to gossip or reveal secrets. Your friends must know you can be trusted and you will be a confidant on their behalf as needed. If not, there can be huge consequences.

Finally, it says where there's no counsel, the people fall. But in the multitude of counselors there is safety. You need to be available to counsel as God speaks to you, as well as receive counsel with an open heart.

I pray today that your God-given faith would allow you to control your tongue, promote faith and be a friend.

Ask Yourself: How will I use my words today?

The Heart Of Christ

Bible Reading: John 19:33-34

The heart is the most important muscle in our body. It is the muscle that keeps all of our blood flowing throughout our entire body. If the heart fails our life is over.

Jesus was crucified on a cross. Crucifixion was one of the most brutal ways to die. When a person was crucified during this time period, it was a common practice to break the persons legs as he hung on the cross. This allowed the body to sag and the person would eventually die of suffocation. When Christ died, however, his legs were not broken. The Bible tells us in John 19:33, "But when they came to Jesus, and saw that he was dead already, they brake not his legs." They didn't have to touch Jesus because he was dead already. This fulfilled an Old Testament prophecy about Jesus that not one of his bones would be broken.

Jesus died of a broken heart. In John 19:34 we read, "But one of the soldiers with a spear pierced his side, and forthwith came there out blood and water." What is significant about this is that modern research shows us that the water and blood mixture means His heart was literally broken. The chambers of His heart came together and flowed out of Christ's side with blood from one and water from the other. When a rupture of the heart happens like this it is a consequence of supreme mental agony and sorrow. Christ bore the weight of the whole world on His shoulders. He died for the sins of the world. He knew that He was the supreme sacrifice. God the Father couldn't bear to look at Christ as He bore the sin of the world. He could have come down from that cross but He stayed there and died for you and me.

Jesus had His heart broken so that you and I can have a new heart. When you accept Him into your life and ask Him to forgive you of your sins, He gives you a new, clean heart. Will you ask Him to come into your heart today?

Ask Yourself: Do I want a new heart, a fresh start and eternal life in heaven with the Lord?

God Rewards Faithfulness

Bible Reading: I Samuel 17:48-50; I Kings 17:7-16

Are you thinking that you don't have anything to give to God? We all have different talents, abilities and things that He can use. The Bible is filled with stories of people who simply gave God what little they had and God worked miracles. He wants us to be faithful with what we have, just as God is faithful in all that He does.

The story of David and Goliath is a classic tale of how God can beat all the odds when someone is faithful. When no one from Israel's army was willing to fight Goliath, David stepped forward and told Saul that God would help him defeat the giant. Saul thought he needed protection. He put a helmet on David's head, armor on his body and he put a sword in his hand. But David couldn't fight with all of that heavy protection. He was comfortable with just his slingshot and five smooth stones. You probably know what happened. It only took one stone to bring down the blasphemous Philistine.

In I Kings 17:7-16, we read about Elijah and the widow at

Zarephath. Elijah asked her for a drink and some food. She said that she only had a handful of meal and a little oil. Elijah promised her that God would provide if she shared it with him. She gave what she had and God multiplied the food. It fed her, her son and Elijah for many days.

Imagine what God can do if we give Him all that we have. If we trust Him with our time, money, possessions and our talent, He will surely honor our faithfulness and do great and mighty things beyond our wildest imagination.

Ask Yourself: Where did my talents and my possessions come from? Do they really belong to me or to God? How can I use what He has provided to honor Him?

How's Your Prayer Time?

Bible Reading: Matthew 6:9-13

If you're like me, prayer, at times, can become a struggle. I have stopped to sit and reflect on my own prayer life and realized that often my prayer life falls short of the amount of time and the quality of time I know I should commit. When this happens, sometimes I go back to the basics. I use the acronym ACTS to help create a structure to help me stay on track.

The A stands for Adoration. It's giving God praise. It's starting your prayer time with just thanking God for who he is, not necessarily what he's done for you. Give him praise for just being God.

The C stands for Confession. You basically sin every day. There's always something that you mess up on and it's so important to take time to ask God for forgiveness for the things you've done wrong. You need to ask him to give you the power, the strength and the encouragement to move forward and not do it again.

The T stands for Thanksgiving. That's the time to thank the Lord for whatever He's done for you, no matter how small. It may be something specific in your family. It may be meeting your financial needs. It may be just the awesomeness of the life that He's given you.

And finally, S stands for Supplication. This is where you take time to ask God for your daily needs and just share with Him your heart. Share the things that are troubling you, the things that you need Him to do for you, and believe He'll do them.

I encourage you to use this ACTS prayer method. It's a great tool to practice learning the foundations of prayer. And as you do it, I think it will help with the structure you need to be more effective during your prayer time.

Ask Yourself: How will I improve my prayer life?

Faith Without Believing Is Only Hope

Bible Reading: John 14:6; Mark 11:24

If you were hooked up to a faith meter today, what would it read? We always talk about having Fearless Faith, and the way to have that is by believing that Jesus is truly the Son of God and that He died for your sins. Many people say they have faith but they don't really believe that Jesus is the Way, the Truth and the Life, as the Bible says in John 14:6. Faith without believing is only hope. It's like saying, "I hope this is going to happen." In reality, you don't really believe it is.

Faith and believing are different than hope. When you accept Christ into your life your belief lives deep in your heart. When you have Christ in your life you know for certain where you're going when you die. You know that Jesus came to this earth to die for your sins and was resurrected so that you can have eternal life with Him. But Christ did so much more while He was here on earth. He healed the blind. He raised the dead. He fed thousands with just a little bread and some fish. When you have faith and believe He can do anything then you move beyond just hoping that it happens.

True faith comes into play when we pray. Mark 11:24 says, "Therefore I say unto you, What things soever ye desire, when ye pray, believe that ye receive them, and ye shall have them." Jesus taught us to pray for His will but He wants us to pray having total faith that He can answer our prayer. Prayer is the key to heaven but faith unlocks the door. Pray knowing and believing that God will give you the answer!

Ask Yourself: Do I truly have faith that God will answer my prayers or am I just hoping He will?

Faith Needs Humility

Bible Reading: James 4:6-10; Genesis 3:4-5

Pride does not please God. James 4:6-10 actually tells us that God opposes the proud. Pride often keeps people from coming to the Lord. Secular humanism is sweeping the world. Secular humanism is a philosophy that embraces human reason, ethics and philosophical naturalism while specifically rejecting religious belief as the basis of morality and decision-making. Moral relativity is a part of humanism because it basically leaves morality up to the individual. Whatever a person believes is moral is moral. Humanism does not believe in an ultimate truth. According to humanism, an individual only has to answer to himself.

Humanism is really the opposite of Christianity. According to humanism, life revolves around the individual. The individual only has to answer to himself. There is no God to answer to. Each person is their own god. It is the same lie that Satan told Eve in the garden of Eden when he said, Ye shall not surely die: For God doth know that in the day ye eat thereof, then your eyes shall be opened, and ye shall be as gods, knowing good and evil. Genesis 3:4-5.

According to the Bible, God is the ultimate judge of morality, not man. There is moral truth versus moral relativity. We need to humble ourselves and submit to God's truth. This is why we read in James 4:10, "Humble yourselves in the sight of the Lord, and He shall lift you up."

Ask Yourself: Am I living my life according to my truth or God's truth?

Just Do It!

Bible Reading: Exodus 3:11; 4:1-2

Have you ever heard God tell you to do something and you didn't do it? Hey, I'm right there with you. The Lord has spoken to me at various times and for whatever reason I haven't followed through. Fortunately, we're in good company. Moses did the same thing when he heard God directly speak from a burning bush! Moses responded in Exodus 3:11, "Who am I, that I should go unto Pharaoh, and that I should bring forth the children of Israel out of Egypt?" He had no confidence in himself.

What about you? Has God spoken to you to do something and you don't have any confidence that you can actually do it? Maybe that's what's scaring you and keeping you from moving forward and doing what He's asked. Moses didn't stop there. He had excuse after excuse. Moses continued in Exodus 4:1, "But, behold, they will not believe me, nor hearken unto my voice: for they will say, The Lord hath not appeared unto thee." We can all come up with great excuses, can't we? Moses went on to say he wasn't eloquent and couldn't speak publicly.

Finally, God said in verse 2, "What is that in thine hand? And He said a rod." God then showed Moses how that rod would be used to initiate the plagues used to release the children of Israel from bondage. By faith he did what God asked and God used what was available to complete His request.

So, what has God asked you to do? Whatever lack of confidence or excuses you come up with will not stop God from wanting to use you to do what He's asked you to do. He has equipped you and wants you to "look into your hands". He has given you everything you need to fulfill His promise to you and fulfill the requests that He's made. Don't put it off any longer. Listen to God. Be obedient. Believe you can do anything God has asked with the talent He's given you and you'll see victory.

Ask Yourself: What do I have "in my hands" that God can use?

Perseverance

Bible Reading: John 16:33; Romans 5:3-5

I'm sure you have had trials that required you to persevere to get through them. This can happen especially if the Lord called you to do something and you had to keep pushing forward to get it done. Sometimes it only happens with dogged determination.

In John 16:33, the Bible tells us, "These things I have spoken unto you, that in me ye might have peace. In the world ye shall have tribulation: but be of good cheer; I have overcome the world." If you keep your faith pointed in the right direction and keep believing and depending on God to get you through it, you are persevering and you will see results.

I'm going to use an analogy from the Pro Football Draft. Every year NFL teams are looking to pick up the best players available. They're looking for a player that will take direction and have the perseverance to finish each play. Let's consider the position of running back. A team wants a running back that will follow his blockers and wait for the hole to open up. As a pro, he knows to trust his blockers. However, when he is in college, and still learning the game, he may make the cut too soon before the blockers have really opened up the hole. Similarly, we need to learn patience in our spiritual life. In Romans 5:3-5 we read, "And not only so, but we glory in tribulations also: knowing that tribulation worketh patience; And patience, experience; and experience, hope: And hope maketh not ashamed; because the love of God is shed abroad in our hearts by the Holy Ghost which is given unto us."

As we grow in Christ, we learn to trust His direction and to persevere and follow His lead. Live your life with perseverance. If you are lacking it, pray and ask the Lord to give you the perseverance you need.

Ask Yourself: Do I exercise patience and perseverance in my spiritual life?

Moments of Glory

Bible Reading: Luke 2:8-17

Can you imagine the amazing rush of excitement the shepherds must have experienced as they beheld an angel of the Lord? They were just doing their normal job watching their flocks at night when all of a sudden the skies lit up and the glory of heaven was shining everywhere! The angel makes an amazing announcement of the greatest news ever! He tells them that a Savior has been born in the town of David and that they will find him wrapped in cloths and lying in a manger. Then, a great company of angels suddenly appears praising God and announcing that His favor rests on men. Then, as quickly as they appeared, they are gone. Wow!!!!

Chances are that you and I will never witness anything quite as glorious or exciting as a heavenly host of angels in our lifetime. But we do receive what I call "sneak peaks" of glory. Think of how you feel when you watch a glorious sunset or hear an incredible piece of music that stirs your soul. Are you filled with awe and wonder when you stare at a star- filled sky on an exceptionally clear night? If you have ever witnessed the birth of a baby, watched an eagle soar or climbed to the top of a mountain, then you have had a small taste of heaven.

When those moments happen, drink it all in. Think about heaven and how beautifully glorious it will be. And in those moments be quiet enough to listen for God's voice.

Ask Yourself: When was the last time you experienced a "moment of glory" on earth? Did you fully appreciate the wonder and beauty of it? When was the last time you saw a sunrise or sunset?

Help Somebody In Need Today

Bible Reading: James 1:27; Luke 14:13-14

I was in Lowe's the other night to purchase something I needed. I looked down a side aisle and noticed a lady riding a mobile cart and realized she wasn't able to get around very well. I saw her looking up at the wall of tools and recognized her dilemma. I quickly went around a couple aisles to get in front of her and asked if she needed help.

I proceeded to pull down the different tool options and helped her look them over without getting up. She decided on one, put it in her basket and then said, "Let me get out of your way so you can get in here and get what you were looking for." I replied, "I'll be honest. I wasn't looking for anything here. I just came over to help you." She was so moved and touched by that and seemed very appreciative. It was such a simple thing, but it made me realize how important simple things can be.

James tells us that the purest form of religion before God is when we help people like orphans and widows, who cannot help themselves. It reinforces to us the importance of helping the needy, doing something for somebody who can't do something in return.

Luke 14:13 re-emphasizes this by telling us when you give a feast invite the poor, the maimed, the lame and the blind and you'll be blessed because they can't repay you. However, it finishes by saying we will be repaid at the resurrection.

I encourage you to go out today and keep your eyes open for somebody to help. That's pure religion and pleases God. Your reward might be a big smile or you might not receive anything until you reach eternity. Help somebody in need today!

Ask Yourself: Who can I help that cannot return the favor?

I Will Give You Hidden Treasures

Bible Reading: Isaiah 45:3

California is known for its beautiful beaches, palm trees, mountains, redwoods, wine and entertainment. But, it is also known for earthquakes, wild fires and mass shootings. Many of us know people whose lives have been turned upside down by one or more of these horrific events. They are devastated and are looking for an answer to the questions, "Why me? Why my family?"

In the book of Isaiah, there's an account about King Cyrus and a promise that God made to him. Isaiah 45:3 tells us that the Lord said, "And I will give thee the treasures of darkness, and hidden riches of secret places, that thou mayest know that I, the Lord, which call thee by thy name, am the God of Israel." When I read this, I see that God has given us hidden treasures that are in places that we're not even looking for.

During times of sorrow and grief, there are hidden treasures that God has for you. This is not just for people living in California. It's for people everywhere. Things happen every day that affect your life and your family. We saw it firsthand when Beth Wheeler passed away. We grieved and were extremely sorrowful, but out of that grief and sorrow God formed Fearless Faith Ministries.

There is hidden treasure in everything that God has His hand on. Pray and seek out the hidden treasure that God has for you in your time of grief and mourning and during times when things just aren't going your way. Pray and look for that hidden treasure, because it's there. Ask God to show you the hidden treasure and in His time He will.

Ask Yourself: Do I seek God during times of sorrow and ask Him to reveal His hidden treasure for me?

Tired of Waiting?

Bible Reading: Isaiah 40:31; Ecclesiastes 3:1; Galatians 5:22

We live in an instant society. We receive our news almost as soon as it happens. Today's news is old before tomorrow even arrives. Coffee machines now brew coffee in a minute. Sending things through the mail is becoming out of fashion because we can now send a text and communicate with someone instantly. I believe that all of this instant access has caused us to become increasingly "impatient." When we want something, we want it NOW!

In Galatians 5:22, we read that patience is a virtue. It is a very difficult virtue to acquire because we want things to happen according to our timing. But our timing is not God's. His timing is perfect!

In Ecclesiastes 3:1 we read that there is a time for everything. Everything includes whatever it is you have been praying about. God promised Abraham and Sarah that they would have a baby and that He would make a great nation from that child. They waited and waited and finally when

Abraham was 100 and Sarah was 90 they gave birth to Isaac! The children of Israel wandered in the desert for 40 years before they entered into the promised land. Joseph spent several years in jail for something he didn't do until Pharoah made him second in command over all of Egypt.

God always answers our prayers. His answer is either yes, no or not now. The last answer is the hardest for us to deal with. Remember that God's timing is not just good, it is perfect. In God's time you will receive your answer.

Ask Yourself: Do I have enough faith to totally trust that God will work out my situation in His perfect time?

Turn Despair Into Hope!

Bible Reading: Lamentations 3:1-26

Do you have those days where everything's going wrong; you're in despair and you want to have a pity party? I think we've all been there. Maybe you're there today. I've got good news to share with you. You are not alone.

The third chapter of Lamentations tells us about a pity party that Jeremiah had.

In the first twenty verses he shares every negative thought that came to his mind and how God was not with him. You might feel like Jeremiah felt that day. He talks about being afflicted by the rod and walking in the darkness. He basically felt like God had not only abandoned Him but that He actually turned on him. He was filled with bitterness and woe.

Okay Jeremiah, we get it! Wow. Talk about despair. But wait! Listen to verse twenty-one, "This I recall to my mind, Therefore have I hope." As soon as Jeremiah thought about the positive things the Lord had done for him, everything changed.

Jeremiah goes on to say in Lamentations 3:22-23, 25-26, "It is of the Lord's mercies we are not consumed, because his compassions fail not. They are new every morning: great is thy faithfulness. (verse 25) The Lord is good unto them that wait for him, to the soul that seeketh him. It is good that a man should both hope and quietly wait for the salvation of the Lord."

Jeremiah's entire demeanor turned around once he remembered everything that the Lord had done for him. I encourage you to do that today. If you're in despair, remember the Lord's mercies. Remember His compassion, it's new every morning. Remember His faithfulness to you. Remember His goodness to you.

There is hope if you'll wait quietly. Don't be in despair. Trust God. Look for His mercies, His compassion, His goodness and His hope.

Ask Yourself: What has God done for me that can bring me hope?

Do You Have an identity Crisis?

Bible Reading: Genesis 1:27; John 1:12-13

There is a major identity crisis in the world today. People are losing touch with who they really are. You see it on social media where many are trying to portray themselves as somebody they are not. There is a desire to portray one's life as exciting and glamorous all the time. Then we have the big question of gender. We are no longer referring to men and women, we are simply referring to people. It's just crazy. We are devaluing the individual by calling them a person not a man or woman. The way things are going we will soon refer to a person as an "It."

People may be confused about who they are but God is not. He says that you and I are His children. In John 1:12-13 we read, "But as many as received Him, to them gave He power to become the sons of God, even to them that believe on His name." But Satan doesn't want us to identify with God even though God tells us we were created in His image. From magazines to television to movies and books, there's constant pressure to drop any reference to a person's sex. It's everywhere today and we are in the thick of it. Satan doesn't want you to see that you are a child of God. He doesn't want us to identify with the fact that He created us as men and women. He wants us to identify as an "It."

I was recently listening to a song on The Imperials' *Heed The Call* album called *Praise the Lord*. There's a verse in the song that says, "Now Satan is a liar and he wants to make us think that we are paupers when he knows himself we are children of the king." That line describes the world today and the society that we live in. It reminds you and me that we are individuals and that we are children of the King of the Universe.

In Genesis 1:27, the Bible tells us "So God created man in his own image, in the image of God created he him; male and female created he them." Apart from our Creator we don't know who we are. When we realize that God created us in His image then we truly realize who we are and why we were put on this earth.

Ask Yourself: Do I realize that the God of the Universe is my Father? Have I found my true identity in Him?

He's in Your Boat!

Bible Reading: Mark 4:35-41

Have you ever been caught in a storm that totally took you by surprise? Perhaps the morning skies were clear and the sun was shining when you left your house. Suddenly, the skies turned dark and before you could react you were in the middle of a drenching downpour without an umbrella! I'm sure this has happened to all of us at one time or another.

There is a story in the Bible about a fierce storm that seemed to come out of nowhere. It is found near the end of the fourth chapter of the Gospel of Mark. Jesus had been teaching a great multitude of people for a long time. Late in the day, Jesus sent the multitude away. Jesus and the disciples got into a boat to sail across the sea to the other side. In Mark 4:37 we read, "And there arose a great storm of wind, and the waves beat into the ship, so that it was now full." The disciples started freaking out but Jesus was actually asleep. The disciples woke Him up and asked Him if He was concerned about the fact that they might perish. Jesus rose up and rebuked the wind and told the sea to be still. The wind ceased and there was a great calm. Jesus then turned to the disciples and asked them why they were so fearful.

No matter what kind of storm you are facing today, Jesus is in the boat with you. He hasn't left you and He never will. He can calm the storm that you are facing in an instant. You just have to place your trust in Him.

Ask Yourself: Am I more focused on the storm I am facing or on Jesus' presence in my life?

We Need Accountability
and Encouragement

Bible Reading: Proverbs 27:17; Romans 5:3-4

If we were standing face to face and I told you I have been a member of a gym, working out fairly regularly for over 20 years, you might question me based on my appearance. I concede this is not a body that you would expect for someone who lifted weights for over 20 years. Apparently there have been a couple things I may have come up short on.

First, I don't have someone to workout with regularly. Which means I don't have someone to encourage me, to motivate me, to make sure I am on time and show up every day. The lack of accountability makes seeing results SO much harder to achieve.

Second, apparently I have an aversion to pain. I take the path of least resistance once my body starts hurting. Who wants to be in pain? I stop short or quit right when I am at the point of doing what I need to do in order to see results.

Unfortunately, sometimes we do the same thing in our

spiritual lives. We all need to be accountable to someone in our spiritual walk. For instance, if you don't attend a good Bible believing church you need to begin. If the church has small groups, you should try to be a part of one. It would allow you to get to know people and create some accountability. You need somebody to ask the hard questions, help encourage and motivate you to stay on the right path. Proverbs 27:17 says, "Iron sharpeneth iron."

Who likes pain? Romans 5:3-4 says, "And not only so, but we glory in tribulations also: knowing that tribulation worketh patience: And patience, experience; and experience, hope:" If you back off once you face a little tribulation, or a little resistance and you aren't willing to fight through it, you're going to stay where you've always been. Let's resist tribulation and pain and move forward in the Lord.

Ask Yourself: What can I do to grow my "spiritual" muscles today?

What Does Losing Weight Have To Do With It?

Bible Reading: I Peter 5:8

About a year ago, I decided I needed to lose weight. The scale told me that I was heavier than I had been in many years, so I found a diet plan that I believed in and started following it. I was very excited that it worked! I lost the excess pounds in a reasonable amount of time. However, after I reached my goal, I stopped following the diet and I gained back every single pound. Since it worked once before, I did it again. This time I lost 60 pounds! The biggest difference, however, is that I have maintained the weight loss and kept it off for over three years. The key to my success is that I now write down everything I eat throughout the day. This keeps me accountable to my diet and I now get regular exercise so I am burning calories in a healthy way.

I find many parallels between our physical health and our spiritual health. When we accept Christ, it's easy to think that all of our problems are over. We think that our heart has been fixed, so Satan won't try to come after us. That's the farthest thing from the truth. I Peter 5:8 tells us, "Be sober, be vigilant; because your adversary the devil, as a roaring lion, walketh about, seeking whom he may devour:"

You have to maintain your spiritual life just like you do your physical life. You do this by reading your Bible and praying daily. It is also a good idea to keep a journal of what God is showing you. When you do, you grow in strength and wisdom. When Satan's attacks start coming, you will have the power to fight back. When you learn key verses in the Bible, you can use those verses to defend yourself against the devil's temptations. When Satan tried to tempt Jesus, Christ quoted scripture to him. Satan can't fight the truth and the Bible is filled with the truth.

As I've maintained my eating habits, I've actually started losing more weight. As I've maintained my spiritual strength, I've become stronger in my faith and my knowledge of the Word. You will too!

Ask Yourself: Am I working on my spiritual health every day?

Child-like Greatness

Bible Reading: Matthew 18:1-4

Jesus' disciples wanted to know who was the greatest in the kingdom of heaven. Jesus shocked them with His answer. He called a little child and told them that whoever became humble like a small child would ultimately be the greatest in the kingdom of heaven. I'm sure this was not the answer they were expecting!

Why do you think Jesus told them to become like a child? Maybe because it is easier to believe when we are children. A child has pure and simple faith. It is easy for a child to experience pure joy in the smallest things. As adults, we complicate things. We tend to associate greatness with accomplishments. As children, we find joy in our experiences.

My grandchildren learned to jump off the diving board into the deep end of my pool with Papa waiting to catch them. They trusted me to keep them safe before they even knew how to swim. They had enough faith to jump into the deep water because they knew that I would catch them. That is the kind of faith God requires of us. We may not know what the future holds, but we know He holds the future. When we demonstrate that simple, childlike faith in our Heavenly Father, He can accomplish great things through us. That is why Jesus told His disciples that the greatest in the kingdom of heaven is the one who is humble enough to become as a little child. God wants us to have simple, childlike faith.

Ask Yourself: Have I humbled myself to trust my Heavenly Father with simple, childlike faith?

Do You Love Like Christ?

Bible Reading: Matthew 5:40-48

Apparently, I got a little prideful this weekend and felt God put me in my place. It was a busy weekend. I made a long drive to my brother's house, spent the day helping him paint, and then had that same long drive back home. The next day, I took the day off to help move my father-in-law from one location to another.

I thought to myself, two out of three days I helped other people! While I was busy patting myself on the back, I felt God check me, saying, "Whoa, let's lower that pride a notch." Then he reminded me of a verse of scripture from the Sermon on the Mount. Matthew 5:46 tells us, "For if ye love them which love you, what reward have ye? Do not even the publicans do the same?" God is setting the bar pretty high, right? As I read that scripture, I realized that I might have been thinking I was some great Christian because I helped people who I love and who love me. However, God is asking me to do far more than that.

The real challenge is in the forty-fourth verse of chapter five where it says, "But I say unto you, Love your enemies, bless them that curse you, do good to them that hate you, and pray for them who despitefully use you, and persecute you." That's where true Christianity and love come in. Can you do that?

Maybe you need to do something as a favor for somebody today, even though you don't get along with the person very well. That's the height that God wants you to reach for as you move forward in your walk with Him. I encourage you to find somebody that you don't know well, or necessarily love, and do something special for them that you wouldn't normally do.

Remember, Jesus healed the ear of one of the soldiers that came to take Him to be crucified. That's the kind of threshold level Jesus sets for you. Let's look for those opportunities to really show true love.

Ask Yourself: Who can I show true love to today?

Fire In Your Belly

Bible Reading: Revelation 3:15-16

Have you ever felt a fire in your belly? Was it a good feeling or a bad one? It was good if it pushed you to be all that you can be. It should be a flame that keeps you going and gives you purpose and energy. It was evil if it was something that just burned you up inside. What type of fire is in your belly today? In Revelation 3:15-16 we read, "I know thy works, that thou art neither cold nor hot: I would thou wert cold or hot. So then because thou art lukewarm, and neither cold nor hot, I will spew thee out of my mouth."

God wants you to be on fire for Him. He wants you to love one another and show grace and forgiveness. He wants you to be like Jesus. He doesn't want you to be a lukewarm Christian who simply goes through the motions. Now is the time to fulfill Christ's greatest commandment that we are to love others as He has loved us. That love should be what fuels the fire in your heart and in your belly. It should be a passion.

It should be a burning inside that moves you to witness to others about the never-ending love of Christ.

Do you have a passion to share Christ with others? God desires for you to be on fire for Him. That's why He sent the Holy Spirit to the people gathered in the upper room. The Holy Spirit appeared as fire coming down from heaven and this ignited a passion in the disciples to share the Good News of Jesus Christ. Do you have that fire in you today? If not, pray that God gives it to you. Let that fire fuel you forward not burn you up. Let it burn brightly for all of the world to see! They will know you're a Christian by your love.

Ask Yourself: Do I have a fire in my belly to share the Good News of Jesus Christ with everyone around me?

Give God Your Gifts

Bible Reading: I Kings 17:7-14; John 6:1-13

The Bible is filled with stories of miracles that involved God asking someone to give the little that they had. The result was God multiplied their gifts to do great things. Let's focus on two such miracles that teach us the importance of using what we have for God's kingdom.

In I Kings 17:7-14, we read that God sent Elijah to hang out by the brook Cherith during a drought in the land. While he was there, God provided food for him through the ravens. They brought him bread and meat in the morning and evening and he drank water from the brook.

The brook eventually dried up because of the lack of rain. God told him to go to a place called Zarephath. He was met at the city gate by a widow gathering sticks for a fire. Elijah asked her for a drink of water and a morsel of bread. She could handle the water, but she told him that she only had a handful of meal and a little oil. She had planned on going home and making a little bread from it so that she and her son could eat it and then die. Elijah told her that the God of Israel said that if she made him a small piece of bread first that the barrel of meal and the oil would last until the Lord sent rain again. The widow did as Elijah asked and the barrel of meal and the oil lasted many days and they all had plenty to eat.

In John 6:1-13 we read about how a great multitude followed Jesus up a mountainside. Phillip asked the Lord how they would feed all of the people. Andrew told Jesus that a small boy had five small barley loaves and two small fish. He gave them to Jesus and five thousand people were fed. Not only that but the disciples gathered up five baskets of food afterward.

God uses the smallest gifts to accomplish great things. All we have to do is give Him what we have.

Ask Yourself: What gifts do I have that I can give to God?

How To Deal With Difficult People

Bible Reading: II Timothy 2:23-24; Romans 12:18

Do you have a difficult person in your life? Difficult people seem to be everywhere. I have trouble watching television for any length of time. For some reason, everyone feels the need to argue their opinion and how they're right and someone else is wrong.

Maybe you have people in your workplace that have strong opinions about the company, politics or whatever it might be. Maybe it's in your own home. Heaven forbid it would be in your church! Unfortunately, there will always be difficult people in our lives.

What does the Bible tell us about how to deal with difficult people? In II Timothy 2:23-24 we are instructed to avoid foolish and unlearned questions, as they only cause strife. That's one reason that Fearless Faith discourages people from getting too political or argumentative on our social media sites. That's not why we're there. We're not there to argue or start fights. We're there to encourage and support.

Timothy goes on to say that as servants of the Lord we must not strive or fight, but be gentle and kind to everyone, able to teach and be patient with difficult people.

There's your "marching orders" today. Be kind to everyone. Can you do that, and be patient with difficult people? Look at a difficult person as your challenge for the day. Show them that you're going to be kind and patient with them. Let them see something different about you and the way you treat them.

Finally, Paul tells us in Romans 12:18, "if it be possible, as much as lieth in you, live peaceably with all men." Let's face it, it's not always possible, but your challenge is if it depends on YOU, you're going to live at peace with everybody. There are difficult people out there, but let's do what the Bible tells us and make them our friends.

Ask Yourself: How will I deal with difficult people today?

What Is The Soul?

Bible Reading: Genesis 2:7; Matthew 10:28

What exactly is the soul? I started researching the Bible for clues. I discovered that in Genesis 2:7 it reads, "And the Lord God formed man of the dust of the ground, and breathed into his nostrils the breath of life; and man became a living soul." Our souls were breathed into us by God and it all started with Adam. God breathed into Adam's nostrils and he became a living soul, which means the soul is a part of our body that is eternal. It's the part of the body that lives on after the body dies and decays. In Matthew 10:28, Jesus said "And fear not them which kill the body, but are not able to kill the soul: but rather fear him which is able to destroy both soul and body in hell." So, the soul lives on after the body dies.

Many years ago, I attended my grandfather's funeral with my parents. I remember dad saying, "I don't want to leave tonight. I don't want to leave him alone. My mom replied, "It's all right, he's not here. His body is just a shell." A few years later, when my dad passed away, I was the last one to leave the funeral home. My Uncle John came in to get me and I told him the same thing. I didn't want to leave my dad by himself. My uncle looked at me and said, "That's not your dad. That's just a shell. His soul is gone." And it hit me. His body was lifeless because his soul was gone.

God told the prophet Jeremiah that He knew him before he was even formed in his mother's womb. God knew his soul even before he was born. Our soul is the part of our body that communicates with God. It's His breath. It's His life and it's what communicates with Him.

Ask Yourself: Do I know where my soul is going when I leave this world?

Everything You Do Today Has a Purpose

Bible Reading: Acts 24:27

I was mowing my lawn one morning thinking how mundane a job it was. There must be a better use of my time. Shouldn't I be doing something more productive then just mowing the lawn? It made me stop and think about how at anytime, wherever we are, whatever we're doing, we can be productive and fulfill our God given purpose.

It reminded me of Acts 24:27 where it tells us that Paul had been in prison for two years for no justifiable reason. It's interesting that Paul didn't appear to get offended or upset. He knew God didn't make mistakes. Wherever Paul found himself, he knew God had a reason and purpose.

You might ask why God didn't continue to expand Paul's incredible missionary work during those two years. He was so full of the Holy Spirit and used by God to evangelize and reveal God's truth. Why would God have left him in a prison for two years? The key is to remember that God has a plan and purpose for every day of your life, no matter how mundane you think it may be. You don't know what impact you can have on the one or two people God puts in front of you. God has you where you are today for a reason.

It doesn't matter what's on your agenda, there's a reason for it. Just as Paul maintained his attitude and was able to impact the kingdom in that prison for two years, you can make an impact where you are right now. Paul influenced leaders, encouraged other believers, wrote letters to his church plants and shared his testimony during that time. I decided to use my time mowing to pray for my family and meditate. Don't underestimate your purpose. Look at everything you do as an opportunity to further the Kingdom of God and fulfill God's plan for you today.

Ask Yourself: What does God want to do with my life today?

The Holy Spirit Regenerates
and Empowers

Bible Reading: Genesis 1:2, 2:7; John 20:21-22; Acts 1:8

The Spirit of God is mentioned in the second verse of the Bible as being there in the very beginning. Genesis 1:2 says, "And the Spirit of God moved upon the face of the waters..." In the second chapter of Genesis we read how God breathed the breath of life into man's nostrils. The Hebrew word for spirit used in both of these verses is "ruach." This word can mean "wind", "breath" or "spirit." It is interesting that it is used to describe the Holy Spirit during the creation of nature and man. It is the "life giving force."

But the Holy Spirit has many functions throughout scripture. The same word is used in John 20:22 when Jesus appeared to the disciples in the upper room after His resurrection from the dead. After He tells them that He is sending them into the world to preach the gospel he "breathes" (ruach) on them and then tells them to receive the Holy Spirit (ruach).

The Holy Spirit can generate and regenerate. It is God's life giving force. It can also empower, as we see in Acts 1:8 where we read, "But ye shall receive power, after that the Holy Ghost is come upon you: and ye shall be witnesses unto me both in Jerusalem, and in all Judaea, and in Samaria, and unto the uttermost part of the earth."

Think of it! The Holy Spirit brings God's regenerating power into our lives. He helps us to be witnesses of God's grace and mercy to everyone we come in contact with. We have to keep ourselves open to His work in our lives every day. When we do, He can accomplish great things in our life through His life in us. Jesus sent the Holy Spirit so that we can tap into His divine power and lead overcoming lives that accomplish great things for God's kingdom.

Ask Yourself: Do I realize that the Holy Spirit is literally God's life giving force living inside of me?

The Holy Spirit is the Life of God in Us!

Bible Reading: Romans 8:15-16; Romans 8:26; John 14:16-18; Acts 2:3

C. S. Lewis said, "The whole purpose for which we exist is to be taken into the life of God." How does this happen? The Holy Spirit makes it happen. He actually brings us into the family of God. In Romans 8:15-16 we read, "For ye have not received the spirit of bondage again to fear; but ye have received the Spirit of adoption, whereby we cry Abba Father. The Spirit itself beareth witness with our spirit, that we are the children of God."

The Holy Spirit is the living presence of God in us. According to Romans 8:26, He helps us to pray when we don't know how to pray. He actually makes intercession for us to the Father. In John 14:17 we read that the Holy Spirit dwells with us and will be with us. In this portion of scripture Jesus is telling his disciples that when He leaves them He will send the Holy Spirit to comfort them. Finally, in Acts 1:8,

Jesus promised the disciples that the Holy Spirit would give them power to take the gospel of Jesus Christ to the world.

Think about how important the Holy Spirit is and should be in your life. He brings you into the family of God. He is the presence of the living God in your life. He comforts you in times of sorrow and He is your source of power to help you accomplish the will of the Father. Finally, the Holy Spirit convicts us and then cleanses us of our sins. He is the refining fire that prepares our hearts and our minds as we worship God.

Ask Yourself: Am I utilizing all that the Holy Spirit is doing in my life? Am I melting away my impurities so that I can truly be the man or woman that God wants me to be?

Heavenly Minded

Bible Reading: Colossians 3:2; Matthew 6:19-20; Psalm 19:1; 2 Peter 3:13

Have you ever heard someone say, "The Bible says you can be so heavenly minded that you're no earthly good?" Well, guess what? The Bible does not actually say that. In fact, it says just the opposite. Colossians 3:2 says, "Set your affections on things above, not on things on the earth." Matthew 6:19 tell us to "lay up for ourselves treasure in heaven." The Bible tells us to keep our minds on heaven.

When my wife was in her final days on earth, her eyes were fixed on a corner of the ceiling in our bedroom. I asked her what she was seeing and she said, "heaven!" When I asked her if it was beautiful, she said, "Yes!!!" She didn't want to take her eyes off of heaven. I honestly believe that God was letting her see it so that she would be excited to go. She told us that she was sad to leave us but that she was not afraid. You see she knew and saw where she was going!

I often think about heaven when I stare into the sky on a

clear night. Many times I can see the big and little dippers, Orion and the Milky Way. It is truly awe-inspiring. When I see a glorious sunset I think that if the earth is this beautiful how amazing will heaven be? I believe God gives us "glimpses of His glory" so that we look forward to being with Him for eternity.

Runners know that it is important to keep their eyes on the finish line during a race. In the same way, if we keep our eyes on heaven, we'll be able to say like my late wife did, "I am not afraid to die.

Ask Yourself: Am I afraid to die or am I excited to go to heaven?

Fearing God

Bible Reading: Deuteronomy 6:24; Psalm 33.18-19; Psalm 103:11

I grew up thinking that God was a big thumb in the sky. If I did something wrong, if I said something wrong, if I did anything that was considered a sin, I was going to hell. I truly believed that. I thought I could not make one mistake or His thumb was going to come down and crush me.

It is just amazing how many people think like this, and they believe this because the Bible tells us to fear God. In Deuteronomy we have the account of the Israelites leaving Egypt. Deuteronomy 6:24 tell us, "And the Lord commanded us to do all these statutes, to fear the Lord our God, for our good always, that he might preserve us alive, as it is at this day."

In Psalms 33:18-19, David tells us, "Behold, the eye of the Lord is upon them that fear him, upon them that hope in his mercy; To deliver their soul from death, and to keep them alive in famine." And he says again a little bit later in Psalm

103:11, "For as the heaven is high above the earth, so great is his mercy toward them that fear him." The Bible reminds us time and again to fear the Lord.

However, this is something very different from my notion of the" Big Thumb in the Sky." It's really the fear that we are going to fail Him. I believe that's what the scripture means by fearing the Lord. Fearing that we are not giving Him 100%; that we are letting Him down. We all fail Him daily but we don't want to because we do fear Him. Thankfully, God is sovereign and just to forgive us. We don't have to fear His thumb anymore. If you have asked Jesus to forgive you of your sins and you have a personal relationship with Him then you never have to be afraid of Him, even when you fail.

Ask Yourself: Am I afraid of God or do I fear failing Him?

You CAN Be Used of God!

Bible Reading: I Corinthians 2:1-5

Do you think that God can't use you? You just don't have the confidence that He's given you any ability, or something to say, to further God's Kingdom?

Let me remind you of Paul, the writer of most of the New Testament and one of the greatest missionaries that ever existed. In talking to the church of Corinth in 1 Corinthians 2:1 he conceded that he didn't come with excellency of speech or of wisdom. Incredibly, Paul did not feel confident in his speaking abilities. He went on to say in I Corinthians 2:3, "And I was with you in weakness, and in fear, and in much trembling". Wow! That's how he approached the church. THAT'S the confidence level he had in himself.

Paul continues by saying in I Corinthians 2:4-5, "And My speech and my preaching were not with enticing words of man's wisdom, but in demonstration of the Spirit and of power: That your faith should not stand in the wisdom of men, but in the power of God". He didn't come in his own strength. He knew in his own strength he was weak. He came in the power of the Spirit and that's what you can do. You don't have to approach God's plan for your day in your own strength. I promise if you seek the power and the strength of the Spirit, He will use whatever abilities you've been given.

If you don't feel you have anything to offer God, then you're only kidding yourself. If you ask for the power of the Holy Spirit in your life and then open yourself up to be used, He WILL use you. Listen to His voice and be obedient. He will use you starting today. Don't think you can't help the kingdom because you can and God wants to do it through you.

Ask Yourself: What can I do for God today, powered by the Holy Spirit?

How to Pray

Bible Reading: I Thessalonians 5:17; Matthew 6:5-13; Luke 11:1-4

It is surprising to me how many people do not seem to understand prayer. Prayer is simply a two-way conversation between you and God. You should talk to God and then listen as He speaks to you through His Holy Spirit and His Word. It is not something that you leave for someone else to do. The Bible tells us in I Thessalonians 5:17 that we should "Pray without ceasing." In other words, we should be in a constant state of prayer. Our conversation with God should happen all day long.

Jesus gave us an example of how to pray in Matthew 6:5-13 and Luke 11:1-4. He warned the disciples to not be like hypocrites who pray so that they can be seen and heard by men. Instead, He tells them in Matthew 6:6 that they should close their door and pray in secret. After all, our prayers are not to other humans but to God.

I have always thought that two of the most powerful

words a person can pray are "thank you." It is important to come to God with an attitude of gratitude for all that He has done for you. I like to start by thanking Him and praising Him for His goodness.

You are probably familiar with "The Lord's Prayer." It is found in Matthew 6:9-13 and Luke 11:1-4. He starts by addressing God as "Father." He then honors Him by saying that His name is holy. Jesus teaches us to humble ourselves by submitting to God's will on earth and in heaven. He then teaches us that it is ok to ask for our daily bread, forgiveness of our sins and deliverance from temptation and evil.

The most important thing about prayer is that it needs to be done in faith. You must truly believe that God hears you and that He will answer your prayers according to His will and in His timing.

Ask Yourself: How much time do I spend in prayer every day? Am I honoring God by talking to Him and asking for His help throughout the day?

Bless the Lord, Oh My Soul!

Bible Reading: Psalm 103

The first verse of Psalm 103 gives you your instructions for the day. It reads, "Bless the Lord, O my soul: and all that is within me, bless His holy name." You need to start your day by praising and blessing God. David goes on to tell us in verse to, "forget not all of His benefits." He forgives all of your sins. Whatever you've done He's forgiven you. He heals all your diseases. If you're sick today, He's the one that can heal you. If you've been sick in the past and have been healed, He was the one who did it.

God redeems your life from destruction. The enemy wants to steal, kill and destroy you and Christ has saved you from that. He crowns you with loving kindness and mercy. His mercies are new for you every morning. He's kind to you. He satisfies your mouth with good things. Stop and think about the good things that the Lord has done in your life and how He's satisfied you.

The Lord is merciful and gracious, slow to anger and

abounds in mercy. He loves you so much. He hasn't dealt with you according to your sins or punished you according to what you deserve. He is worthy to be blessed and praised. I want to encourage you to do just that.

Think about all that He's doing in your life and just take a moment right now to pray, "Father, I do bless your holy name. I thank you for your goodness to me; I thank you for forgiving me of ALL my sins. Lord, the mercies that you show me are new every morning. I ask you to meet my needs today. I can never praise you enough for all you do for me. I ask you to do great things today. Amen."

Ask Yourself: Will I take time to bless and honor the Lord today?

Jesus: The Reason for the Bible

Bible Reading: Hebrews 4:12, John 14:6

As I was reading my Bible, I was thinking about its origin and where it came from. How did we get it, and why is it still available now over two thousand years after Christ was crucified? I realized that the Bible would not exist, if Christ had not come back from the dead. He is not only the focal point of the Bible, He is actually the reason it exists.

The Bible is composed of the Old Testament and the New Testament. The Old Testament is what the Jewish Rabbis of Jesus' time studied. They lived their lives according to the laws of the Torah. But, the Old Testament also pointed to the coming of Christ as the Messiah. So why does the New Testament exist? It's because of Christ's resurrection.

The New Testament is full of eyewitness accounts of people who witnessed the crucifixion of Christ but who also interacted with Him after He rose from the grave. It's because of these witnesses that we have the Bible today. Most of the disciples were martyred for their faith. Many were actually crucified for their faith like Jesus. They would not denounce their faith in Jesus as the Messiah. They witnessed His many miracles of healing. They encountered a living Jesus after they saw Him crucified and buried in a tomb. They couldn't deny it. They were willing to die for their devotion and love for Christ. They knew He was the Savior of the world.

The Bible is still changing lives today because of the relevant message of salvation through faith in Christ. When you read it, you will want to know more about the man who was responsible for it.

Ask Yourself: Do I know the risen Christ as my personal Lord and Savior?

The Certainty of Death

Bible Reading: Psalm 90:12; John 3:16

Death is something that most people don't like to think about. I find myself thinking about it more since my wife passed into heaven. I often say that she taught me how to live and she taught me how to die. She lived her life to the fullest. She truly knew how to squeeze sixty seconds out of every minute. She understood the importance of living in the moment. One of her favorite sayings was, "don't sweat the small stuff." When it came time for her to die, she wasn't afraid. She said that she was sad, but not afraid. She faced death fearlessly, which is part of the reason we named this ministry Fearless Faith.

In Psalm chapter 90, David tells us in verse 12, "So teach us to number our days, that we may apply our hearts unto wisdom." In other words, he thought it was a wise thing to think about how long you will live. When you do you realize that your life isn't very long. It's important to make the most out of every day that God gives us on this earth. Dr. Billy

Graham echoed David's wise words when he said everyone should think about the certainty of their own death.

Sooner or later, death will come to us all. John Donne said that there is a democracy about death, "It comes equally to us all and makes us all equal when it comes." But, it doesn't have to fill us with sadness. On the contrary, it can fill us with joy when we realize that if we have accepted the Lord Jesus Christ as our Savior, and asked forgiveness of our sins, then we will live in heaven with God forever. John 3:16 states this amazing fact by saying, "For God so loved the world, that He gave His only begotten Son, that whosoever believeth in him shall not perish, but have everlasting life." This verse has become known as the salvation verse for it promises the greatest gift anyone can have----eternal life! So don't be down- trodden because God has saved you from hell and offers you an eternity in heaven instead.

Ask Yourself: How long will I live? What will others say about me at my funeral?

Worship God For Who He Is

Bible Reading: Matthew 21:1-11

It's incredible the highs and lows that can take place from one weekend to the next. Let's consider Jesus' last weekend. Palms were used by the people to celebrate what the Jews thought was their new king. They thought He was the one that was going to be their Savior and reign over Israel. They had an abundance of praise and worship for this man Jesus. They didn't really understand or know what it was all about. But they worshipped Him, and in Matthew 21:9 they said, "Hosanna to the son of David; Blessed is He who cometh in the name of the Lord; Hosanna in the highest." The unfortunate thing was these Jews did not see him as their spiritual savior, only as a man that was coming to redeem them from tyranny and give them what they wanted.

Their praise was conditional, as they were looking to *get* something from this man. Their praise was not to honor and glorify the Son of God.

Unfortunately, I'm afraid that's what happens too often

in our lives if we're honest. We praise the Lord with ulterior motives, thinking that there's something in it for us. I encourage you to praise the King of Kings and the Lord of Lords for *who* he is, not for what He can give you. As it turned out, as the week went on, these same Jewish people totally turned their back on Him. They allowed Him to be crucified because He did not appear to be what they wanted Him to be. Don't let that be you today. Acknowledge Christ for who He is. Worship Him and glorify Him as only you can do.

You were created to give praise and glory and honor to the King of Kings. So, think about that today. As you're going through the day, worship the King of Kings for *who* He is and not what he can give you.

Ask Yourself: What is my motive for worshipping God?

The Pharisees Make Me Laugh

Bible Reading: John 11:32-44; 47-48

Christ was traveling between Jerusalem and Galilee shortly before His betrayal. The disciples wanted Jesus to stay out of Jerusalem because they knew that certain people wanted to kill Him. But He decided to go back when He heard about his friend, Lazarus, who had died a couple of days earlier and had already been buried. You have probably heard the story how Jesus raised Lazarus from the dead.

Some of the people that witnessed Jesus raising Lazarus from the dead went to the Pharisees and told them what they had seen. The Pharisees, being the weaklings that they were said, "If we let him thus alone, all men will believe on him: and the Romans shall come and take away both our place and nation." (John 11:48)

You have to wonder why the Pharisees thought that *THEY* could somehow control what Jesus did. Jesus is the Son of God yet they thought they were going to stop Him! Jesus already knew their plan and already knew what was going to happen but they had the audacity to think that they could control Him. The Pharisees were so afraid of what would be taken away from them that they didn't recognize Jesus for who He really was. The Pharisees actually believed their own press and thought they were the righteous ones.

By contrast, Christ was the humble one. He was the one who healed the sick and became their friend. He sincerely loved people. While the Pharisees paraded around and attempted to control their followers, Jesus actually loved them.

We should all aspire to be like Jesus and follow in His footsteps. We need to love one another instead of worrying about losing our status or our possessions. God owns everything and if He wants you to have it, you will have it. Jesus showed us how to live and love others. Be like Jesus not like the Pharisees.

Ask Yourself: Do I resemble Jesus or the Pharisees?

Reach Out to Touch Jesus

Bible Reading: Matthew 9:20-22

There is a brief story near the end of the ninth chapter of Matthew in the Bible. It is about a woman who had an issue with her blood for twelve years. She heard Jesus was in the area and she told herself that if she could just touch Jesus' cloak she would be healed. She actually got close to Jesus and accomplished her goal. Jesus turned around and when he saw her he said, 'Daughter, be of good comfort; thy faith hath made thee whole."

This is a story of great faith. It is interesting that Jesus told her it was her faith that made her whole. When my wife, Beth, was in the final days of her life, a neighbor came over and shared this story with her. The amazing thing was that Beth's issue was also with her blood, but my neighbor didn't know that. He told Beth that Jesus was in the room and if she was ever afraid all she had to do was reach up to touch Him. Her hands were swollen badly from the fluid that had invaded her body. She couldn't lift her hands to wipe a tear from her face. Yet, several times during the course of those last few days we saw her lift her hand straight up in the air.

Faith is powerful. It can heal the sick and comfort the sad. Faith in Jesus restores broken lives. If you haven't put your faith in Him do it today. Reach up to the Lord in faith and ask Him to forgive you of your sins and to cleanse your soul. He will put your life back together and give you hope and a purpose.

Ask Yourself: Do I want my life to be completely whole? Do I have the faith to reach out and touch Jesus just like the woman in Matthew chapter nine?

Spiritual Lifeguard

Bible Reading: Isaiah 41:9-10

Do you ever feel like you are in the deep waters of life? Are you paddling for all you're worth, losing strength, not sure you can get to the other side? That's how my grandson, Sam, felt in a recent swim lesson.

His instructor was right beside him and instructed Sam to swim across the deep part of the pool. Sam was fearfully yelling, "I can't, I can't, I can't!" The instructor, just out of reach, was encouraging him, "Yes you can! You've got this! You're almost there, you're almost there! Keep going, keep going! You're almost there! You made it! Good job!" Before Sam knew it, he had made it to the other side, proud as could be, giving a high five to his instructor.

Maybe you're feeling that way today. Maybe you're in life's deep waters, paddling for all you're worth, saying, "I can't, I can't, I can't." I want to remind you that your lifeguard is right there beside you. You don't have to fear a thing. God is your lifeguard and He's with you every step of the way, cheering you on to the other side.

Don't lose hope today. Let me encourage you with Isaiah 41:9-10, which says, "Thou art my servant; I have chosen you and have not cast thee away. Fear thou not; for I am with thee; do not be dismayed; for I am thy God. I will strengthen thee; yea I will help thee; yea I will uphold thee with the right hand of my righteousness."

God's right there with you. He wants to strengthen you. He wants to uphold you in His right hand. He'll be there. So, whatever you're going through today, however deep the waters, remember God's right there with you. He's helping you all the way, ready to high five you at the end of the journey as He leads you on to the next one.

Ask Yourself: What "deep waters" am I going through that I need to remember God is right beside me?

How to Handle Failure

Bible Reading: Psalm 31:23-24; I John 1:9

We have all failed God. The Bible is filled with stories of people who loved God but failed Him regularly. Adam, Moses, David, Peter and many more all failed God miserably. But the questions isn't how often do you fail God, but what do you do when you fail God? Do you run and hide like Adam and Eve in the Garden of Eden after they sinned and God came looking for them? Or do you repent immediately like David did when he was confronted with his sins? God wants you to draw near to Him when you fail him and not pull away.

You are not perfect and you never will be on this earth. But guess what? You are in good company because even the Apostle Paul said that he failed God daily. We all do and that is the reason we have to constantly ask God for His forgiveness and His help. If we don't then we will keep failing him in the same way over and over again. Ask God to help you to learn how to get past your failures. Ask the

Holy Spirit to help you overcome your areas of weakness, so you don't relive the same failure again and again. I encourage you to read Psalm 31 in the Bible. The last two verses (23 and 24) read, "O love the Lord, all ye his saints: for the Lord preserveth the faithful, and plentifully rewardeth the proud doer. Be of good courage, and he shall strengthen your heart, all ye that hope in the Lord."

When you stumble along the way, pick yourself up and run towards God. You don't have to run away lamenting the fact that you failed again. Run towards Jesus Christ who has forgiven you. Remember that Jesus loves you and did more than anyone could ever do for you by dying on the cross for your sins. He desires to be close to you even when you fail. I John 1:9 reads, "If we confess our sins, He is faithful and just to forgive us our sins, and to cleanse us from all unrighteousness."

Ask Yourself: When I fail God do I run away from Him or toward Him?

Praise in Pain

Bible Reading: Psalm42:5; Psalm 22; Nehemiah 8:10

Pain is inescapable in this world. But there is a way to escape it once we experience it. The answer may surprise you-**Praise!** The Bible says that God inhabits the praises of His people. The more we praise Him for His goodness, the less aware we are of our pain. Praise is the best antidote for the blues. As you praise the Lord your mind and soul begin focusing on His blessings and His goodness. An attitude of gratitude begins to develop.

Russ Taff and the Imperials sang a popular song many years ago called "Praise the Lord." There is a line in that song that says, "For the chains that seem to bind you, serve only to remind you that they drop powerless behind you when you praise Him." This is so true! There is a freedom that occurs when we praise the Lord. It is a freedom from the chains of our problems that bind us and tie us up in knots. Satan knows that if we are overcome with sadness we will be unable to serve the Lord. The devil loves seeing people become defeated by their problems. But the Lord loves seeing people filled with joy. The Bible says, "The Joy of the Lord is your strength!"

You have the choice today to dwell on your problems or to dwell on His goodness. You can focus on what is going wrong or you can focus on what is going right. You can give in to the pain of your problems or you can be an overcomer by praising the Lord and focusing on His goodness!

Ask Yourself: Am I going to dwell on my problems today or will I praise the Lord for all of His goodness?

Offer What You Have To Jesus

Bible Reading: John 6:5-14

When was the last time you felt you gave Jesus everything you had? I realize sometimes I'm not doing that and I need to find out why and correct it. I want to feel like everything I have is available and that God can use it.

The sixth chapter of John tells us about the hungry multitude following Jesus. Jesus asked Philip how they could feed everybody. Philip didn't know and basically that they didn't have enough money to feed all of the people. Andrew told Jesus that there was a boy in the crowd who had five barley loaves and two small fishes.

If you know the story, you know what Jesus did. He blessed the loaves and fish, the disciples then passed them out, and everyone on the hillside was fed. Incredibly, there were twelve baskets of left over pieces. What a miracle--a miracle that couldn't have happened if the little boy had not offered all he had, his two fish and five loaves of bread.

It was interesting to me that out of all those people, a little boy was the only one that offered what he had. I'm certain there was more than one person in that crowd that had food with them. They just didn't offer it. Jesus couldn't use what wasn't offered.

I want to encourage you to offer what you have to Jesus. I don't care if you feel like it's two fish and five loaves of bread among thousands of people. Leave that up to God. God will take what you give him and multiply it for His purposes and the reward will be great.

Are you like the rest of the crowd and not giving the Lord what you should and allowing Him to use it? Maybe it's your talents or maybe it's your money. Whatever it is, I encourage you to release it today and like the little boy did, watch what God does with it.

Ask Yourself: What do I possess that I can give to God?

What Are You Cooking?

Bible Reading: II Timothy 3:16-17

I enjoy cooking. I like to prepare by putting all of my ingredients on the counter. The most important thing I put right in front of me is my cookbook. I want to make sure I get all of the ingredients right. I can improvise all I want but to have the authentic taste means to follow the recipe and use all of the original ingredients.

Once in a while, when I cook a recipe that I am familiar with, I try to prepare it without consulting my cookbook. If I miss an ingredient, or use a wrong measurement, then something doesn't taste right. I then go back to my cookbook and see where I got off track.

My Bible is my life cookbook. I need it to stay on track. I have to read it and study it each day. In II Timothy 3:16-17 we read, "All scripture is given by inspiration of God, and is profitable for doctrine, for reproof, for correction, for instruction in righteousness: That the man of God may be perfect, thoroughly furnished unto all good works."

We all need to use our Bible like a cookbook. We need to check God's recipes for successful living. He has something planned for each and every one of us. We have to be prepared and know how to handle every situation. The only way we are going to do that is by studying and reading His Word daily.

Once you start reading the Bible you will begin to see things that you've never seen before. Try praying this prayer before you start to read: "Lord open up my spiritual eyes. Let me read what You want me to read and let me see what You want me to see." He will guide you and He will reveal Himself to you through His Word.

Ask Yourself: Am I using my Bible to prepare for each day just like I use my cookbook to prepare a great meal?

HELP!!!

Bible Reading: Psalm 46:1-4; Psalm 30:2-3; Isaiah 41:10-13

What do we do when we need far greater help?

Many years ago, I was in a terrible place. I struggled with serious sin and it nearly cost me my life. I was in so much emotional pain, that I struggled to get out of bed. I remember one time when my wife made me get out of bed and go to an important meeting at work. I was over a half- hour late to the meeting and when I got there I had nothing to contribute.

The world had become a scary place to me. I was afraid to leave my home. I had no self- confidence. I even lost my voice and was unable to speak. Eventually, I had to take a five-week medical leave from work. I was on several medications for depression. The worst part of it all was that I felt totally separated from God. I read my Bible and prayed, but I felt like my prayers were just bouncing off the ceiling.

One day, I literally cried out to the Lord for help. I told God that I needed to feel His presence because He promised in His Word that He would never leave me or forsake me.

Something miraculous took place. I felt His presence again. I heard His still small voice say that He was with me and that together we would work our way out of the place I was in. I slowly started to work my way back to a life that was far greater and far richer than I had ever known before.

God will never leave you or forsake you. If you are feeling dead inside and you feel like your life is over, know that it is not. God is not finished with you. He can turn your situation into a thing of beauty. He can pull you out of the darkness and into the light. He will pull you out of the mud and set your feet on solid ground. All you have to pray is, "Help!!!"

Ask Yourself: Do I want to continue to live in fear? Is it time that I cried out to the Lord for help?

The Greatest Hindrance to Experiencing God's Presence

Bible Reading: Ephesians 5:15-16; Psalm 46:10

I'd like to make a recommendation we all take the phrase "I'm too busy" out of our vocabulary. I'm sure we can all (and DO) say we're too busy at times, right? Unfortunately, I think we tend to use that phrase as a crutch sometimes. We each have 24 hours in the day. If we're too busy for certain things in our day, it's probably our own fault. We mistakenly try to do more than is possible in a given day. And, if we're honest, most of us use that phrase as a way to get out of doing something we don't want to do. Does "Oh, I'd love too, but I'm just too busy," sound familiar? I think one of the greatest single threats to us spending time in God's presence is busyness.

Paul writes in Ephesians 5:15-16, "See then that ye walk circumspectly, not as fools, but as wise, Redeeming that time, because the days are evil." Are you redeeming your time?

Are you making your time as beneficial and worthwhile as possible? That's my question to you.

It's easy to be busy, but are you busy with the right things? Think about and prioritize your day. Determine what's most important and work your way down. Secondly, create margin in your day. Don't fill your day with a to-do list so long that you know you'll never get it done. Prioritize the day with the most important things and leave some margin. That is how you will have time to spend in God's presence.

Psalm 46:10 says, "Be still and know that I am God." If you'll start your day seeking His presence and direction as a number one priority, I assure you God's peace will make the busyness of the rest of the day a little more bearable. He can help you determine a more realistic plan for the day. Try it!

Ask Yourself: Have I made time for my true priorities today?

Where Is Your Opportunity?

Bible Reading: I Corinthians 15:58

I don't have enough talent. I'm not quite ready to serve the Lord. I just don't have enough time. When things slow down I'll be able to do more for the Lord. Have you ever used one of these excuses to **not** do something for God? Has He placed something on your heart that won't go away and you know you should be doing it? Don't make any more excuses. Now is the time to step out in faith and do it!

In I Corinthians 15:58, the Bible tells us, "Therefore, my beloved brethren, be ye steadfast, unmoveable, always abounding in the work of the Lord, forasmuch as ye know that your labour is not in vain in the Lord." You will never regret working for God. Your work will make an impact on lives. Ask the Lord to give you guidance and the courage to move forward. There might be an opportunity at your church, your job or in your neighborhood. If God is speaking to you then it is important for you to respond. Today is the day for you to take the first step.

If you want to serve the Lord but don't know what He would have you do just ask Him. Spend time in prayer and then be still and listen for his voice. He can speak to you in many ways but you will know when He does. He will place a desire in your heart to be used of Him. This is how Fearless Faith started. Three good friends felt like God was speaking to us individually to do something for His kingdom and we realized that we could do it together. We started this ministry when we were all in our sixties so **it is never too late.** You will be fulfilled as you do something that has eternal value. Go ahead and take that first step today!

Ask Yourself: What opportunities do I have to serve the Lord today?

Is Worry Ruining Your Life?

Bible Reading: Matthew 6:25-34

Five hundred years ago a man named Michel de Montaigne said, "My life has been filled with terrible misfortune; most of which never actually happened." Wow! Could that be a quote from you? Have you made yourself sick by worrying over things that never happened? Guess what? You are not alone. In a recent study, subjects were asked to write down their worries over an extended period of time. They were then asked to identify which of their imagined misfortunes never happened. The result was that 85% of what they worried about never came to pass! Think of all that wasted energy!

I am convinced that some people like to worry. Have you ever known someone who was constantly worried about something? In the Bible, Jesus tells us to STOP IT! In Matthew 6:25-34, He told his disciples (I'm paraphrasing) to not worry about tomorrow because there is enough to worry about today. He told them that birds don't worry about having enough food because God always provides for them.

He also pointed out that the lilies of the field don't worry about clothes. They just grow into splendor and beauty. His point was that it is a waste of time and energy to worry about things that don't really matter.

Instead of worrying, Jesus told his disciples that they should seek first the Kingdom of God, and His righteousness; and all these things shall be added unto you. You can focus on your problems and worries or you can focus on your Savior who will never leave you nor forsake you. He wants you to have complete trust in Him knowing that He will provide all of your needs.

Ask Yourself: Am I tired of wearing myself out with worry? Isn't it time that I lay all my worries at the foot of the cross?

A Life of Good Works

Bible Reading: Philippians 1:6

I was walking up to the counter at the drug store this week and overheard the checkout person asking an elderly man, "So how are you doing today?" His response was, "I'm above ground." She replied something to the effect, "Well, that's what counts." I wanted so badly to interrupt their conversation and say, "No! No! Life has so much more to offer than just staying above ground."

Who wants to live life just breathing? Who wants to go through the day just to say they made it through the day? There is so much more to life. I recently read a quote by Jim Rohn that said, "Life is not just the passing of time. Life is a collection of experiences and their frequency and their intensity." I agree. We need to fill our lives with God prepared experiences and focus on the quality and intensity of those experiences.

Maybe you find yourself in a rut. Maybe you're just living day by day and trying to get through this one. Could you refocus on a higher meaning for your life? Try to focus on the experience of the day. Be proactive. Have some key experiences that have some intensity to them, something that you're going to remember. Do something that's going to be positive, something that's going to have a God purpose. In doing so, I believe God can change your mindset and how you approach each day. He's going to use you in ways you've not been used before.

Philippians 1:6 says, "Be confident of this very thing, that he which hath begun a good work in you will perform it until the day of Jesus Christ." Be assured that He is not done with you! He has a good work for you to do. He wants you to complete it. Look with fresh eyes at the options of the day, for God has a quality experience He wants you to complete. He doesn't want you to just be "above ground."

Ask Yourself: What quality experience or "good work" will I complete today?

Pray Your Day

Bible Reading: Psalm 32:8; Isaiah 30:21

How many times do you just say a quick prayer over your day and go on your way? Perhaps you don't pray about your day at all. Having a relationship with Jesus means talking to Him every day throughout the day. It means praying over everything in your life. It means praying over things you may think are irrelevant on your schedule. Everything is relevant to God.

Many people have a daily "To Do List." Prayer time should be at the top of each day's list. Make Jesus a part of your day by dedicating a certain amount of time each day to prayer and reading the Bible. Then, pray over each item on your "To Do List" individually. Ask God to let you discern what the most important items are and then give you wisdom on how to handle each situation. He will guide you throughout your day. In Psalm 32:8 we read, "I will instruct thee and teach thee in the way which thou shalt go: I will guide thee with mine eye." In Isaiah 30:21 the Bible says, "And thine ears shall hear a word behind thee, saying, This is the way, walk ye in it, when ye turn to the right hand, and when ye turn to the left."

God will speak to you when you spend time in prayer daily. How do you hear His voice? Ask God to help you to listen. It may be a still small voice within you, or it may be in the things that are happening around you. You'll start to recognize His voice when you pray your day. Things will go more smoothly and your day will be more joyful. You will start to see the good even when things don't seem to go your way. You will see the good that can come out of a bad situation when God is in charge. He will go with you and guide you when you pray your day!

Ask Yourself: Will I begin today to pray my day each and every day?

Jesus Take Over!

Bible Reading: Proverbs 3:5-6; Romans 15:13

Have you ever lost control of your car while driving? Maybe you hit a patch of ice or your car began to swerve and you realized you were heading for danger. The most effective prayer in that instance is, "Help me Jesus!'

You can easily start moving away from God's direction. It can happen gradually. You start spending less time in prayer. Maybe you stop reading your Bible because you don't wake up in time. Soon you start making decisions without asking God for His wisdom and His direction. It doesn't take too long before you realize that you are traveling down a road that you never intended to take. Soon you realize that you are losing control of your life. When you realize that you are on the wrong path cry out to God immediately and ask Him to take the wheel. Ask Him to take over the direction of your life and to give you the strength and the discipline to get back on course.

Don't wait until it is too late and you find that your car is in the ditch.

Today's reading in Proverbs tells us that we need to trust in the Lord with all of our heart and not lean on our own understanding. We need to acknowledge Him in all our ways. That means that we need to be praying about every decision in our lives. And what does He promise when we do this? He promises to direct our paths. When we ask for God's wisdom in all areas of our lives we know that our future will be secure and filled with hope.

Ask Yourself: Am I praying for God's wisdom and leading in every decision of my life?

Does God Like What He Sees In You?

Bible Reading: Genesis 6:5-8

I don't think there is a sadder story in the Bible than the story of Noah. God was so upset with mankind that he chose to destroy everything He had created. How unfortunate and sad.

God saw that evil in humanity was out of control. People thought only evil. They imagined evil. Evil was everywhere from morning to night. God was sorry He had made the human race in the first place. It broke His heart. God said, "I will destroy man whom I have created from the face of the earth.......for it repenteth me (I regret) that I have made them."

However, the story goes on to say that Noah was different. Noah found grace in the eyes of the Lord. In other words, God liked what he saw in Noah. Noah was surrounded by an evil world, just as you are today. He did not let the evil of the world overtake him. He was focused on God. He was obedient to God. He had character and integrity that God wanted and God was pleased with what he saw in Noah.

What if the Bible were still being written today? What if God would look down today and saw all the evil in the world? Would He zero in on you and think he or she is different? Would He like what He saw? What a sobering thought to reflect on today. Is everything you're doing pleasing to God? Are you being obedient to him? Are you walking in integrity? Are you walking and carrying that character that God wants for your life? I pray that you are.

I would ask you to seek to do those things in a greater way because I want God to look down on you in favor as He did Noah.

Ask Yourself: How can I please God in a greater way today?

Sky Pilot

Bible Study: Proverbs 3:5-6

When I was a teenager there was a popular song by Eric Burton and the Animals called *Sky Pilot*. It was about an army chaplain and the young men that were going off to war. Every time I heard that song it reminded me that God is our Sky Pilot.

When we give ourselves to the Lord and ask Him to direct our life, we begin our journey together. When something knocks us off the path, our first reaction is to ask, "Where is God? Has He forsaken me?" There are going to be bumps in the road of life but God will never leave us or forsake us.

When using an automobile guidance system, you never go directly from point A to point B. The guide takes you around accidents, construction zones and traffic jams to get you to your destination as quickly and safely as possible. In the same way, God may take you on detours, as He did the Israelites, but He will always have you where you are suppose to be at the right time.

When traveling by plane, you depend on the pilot to get you to your destination. You literally put all of your faith in him. The same is true when you give your life to the Lord. You're putting all of your faith in Him to get you where you need to be in life. When things seem to start going sideways, the wise thing to say is, "Lord you're in control. I've handed my life over to you and I know that you will get me to my destination safely." Proverbs 3:5-6 says, "Trust in the Lord with all thine heart; and lean not unto thine own understanding. In all thy ways acknowledge Him, and He shall direct thy paths."

When you ask God for guidance, He will always be there. He will guide and direct you as the sky pilot of your life.

Ask Yourself: Am I trusting God to lead and guide me to where I need to go in life or am I still trying to be the pilot of my life?

No More Aches and Pains

Bible Reading: I Corinthians 15:42-44

The greatest athletes of all time eventually have to retire. It is always sad to watch a great competitor slow down and quit the sport they love. I will never forget watching the greatest boxer of all- time, Mohammad Ali, as he tried to pull a comeback against the reigning Heavyweight Champion at the time, Larry Holmes. Ali was in his late 30's and he had lost all of his speed and power. The younger Holmes was able to hit Ali whenever he wanted. He actually had mercy on Ali after a few rounds when it was apparent that Ali wasn't able to block any of Holmes' punches. He wasn't able to throw any either. It was sad to watch the three- time Heavyweight Champion of the World try to hold on way too long.

The fact is Father Time is undefeated against all human beings. Eventually we all age and slow down until our earthly body finally gives out. But the good news is that, as Christians, we know that we will receive a new, glorious body in heaven.

Our new body will never grow old. That is the spiritual body which Paul wrote about in I Corinthians 15: 42-44.

Are you discouraged today due to aches and pains? Are you wondering what happened to your once strong and youthful body? Sooner or later we all grow weaker. We begin to hurt in places where we didn't even know we had places. But this body is just our temporary home. When we get to heaven we will have a glorious, imperishable body that will be better than the one we had on earth in our prime. And we shall spend eternity with the Greatest of All Time----Jesus Christ.

Ask Yourself: Do I thank God for my body and my health or do I just complain about my aches and pains? Somebody is worse off than you are so try to bring "an attitude of gratitude" with you as you crawl out of bed every morning.

If God Can Use Dirt, He Can Use You

Bible Reading: Genesis 2:7; John 9:6-7

When was the last time you felt like you were used by God? Maybe you don't feel like you're *capable* of God using you. Maybe you don't feel like you have the talent or the skill that God can use. I don't believe that and you shouldn't either.

In Genesis, as God was creating the heavens and the earth, it was interesting to me that he made man out of dirt. Many of you have heard the expression dust to dust. We know that He also made all of the animals out of dirt. Out of all that God had available to him, God chose to use dirt to form all that He created.

We look into the New Testament and see in John where Jesus used dirt as well. He mixed dirt with spit and He put it on a blind man's eyes and the blind man was able to see again. It was miraculous. God used dirt for extraordinary things. Jesus used dirt for extraordinary things. (You know where I'm going with this.) If God can use dirt, I promise that He can use you. Open up your mind and your heart and realize that God is capable of using *anything* that's available to Him. I encourage you to become available for God to use.

He wants to use you, but you have to be available and willing to be used. He may have a miracle for you to be part of today. You just have to get over all the roadblocks and the voices in your head that are telling you you're not good enough and that God would never use you. If God can use dirt, He can use you!

Ask Yourself: How will I let God use me today?

A Conference Call With God

Bible Reading: Matthew 18:20; I Thessalonians 5:17

At Fearless Faith we do conference calls because we live in different parts of the country. We can't all be at the same place at the same time very often. We have a conference call to keep everything in order and ensure that we are staying on course in the direction God is leading us. And we use our conference call time to pray together.

Today my wife and I will be making our own conference call. This call won't require a phone because we'll be talking with God. The Bible says in Matthew 18:20, "For where two or three are gathered together in my name, there am I in the midst of them."

God is in our midst when we pray together. When my wife and I take matters before the Lord, we know that He is in our midst. Now that doesn't mean God doesn't hear us when we're praying individually because the Bible tells us in I Thessalonians 5:17 to "Pray without ceasing". We pray throughout the day in our thoughts and in our words, silently or out loud. We're always praying and God hears our prayers.

When God tells us that when two or three are gathered together that He is in our midst, I believe God sees our obedience and faith. We come to Him together because we believe that what He said is true. It is so important to come together and pray in unity. I want to encourage you to do the same today. Set up a conference call with God and someone in your family or a friend or a church member. Get together with a person you have confidence in. Believe that God will hear and answer your prayers. And as God has promised, He will be there with you too. God never misses a conference call from His children.

Ask Yourself: Who comes to mind when I think of praying with someone? Is it time to set up a conference call with God?

Your Plans His Purpose

Bible Reading: Proverbs 19:21; Jeremiah 29:11

A popular country song talks about the fact that many times when we make our plans God starts laughing, because He has other plans. Ultimately, our life and our future are in God's hands, so it is important to ask Him for wisdom and guidance in all of our decisions. God has a specific purpose and specific plan for each of us.

Many times we see the road we are traveling start to bend, and we start to worry because we don't know what is around the bend. We can't see where the road is taking us, but God already knows where it leads. He can see where we came from, where we are and where we are going. He always knows what is around the bend because He knows our entire life's story. He sees the beginning, the middle and the end as well as every stop along the way. We need to have the faith to know that wherever the road takes us, God is already there.

Proverbs 19:21 tells us, "There are many devices in a man's

heart; nevertheless the counsel of the Lord, that shall stand." Do you trust that the Lord has a plan for your life? Do you believe that He will help you get where you need to be?

Trust Him today with all your heart and with all your plans and know that He has a wonderful plan for you!

Ask Yourself: Do I tend to panic when things don't go the way I plan? Or, do I ultimately trust God to work things out for His glory even when my plans fall apart?

Beware of the Little Things

Bible Reading: Song of Solomon 2:15

It's amazing to me that a "little" cold can take over your whole body. It's just a tiny germ. But once that germ gets into your body it affects you completely. That's just the way it is, isn't it? So many times, it's the little things in our lives that affect us the most. I think that's because we don't think something's a big deal so we don't focus on it or worry about it enough.

My wife and I laugh because I have a desk chair in my office that I need to replace. It has a hydraulic lift that slowly leaks throughout the day. It is so subtle I don't realize it until I'm almost to the floor and can't type. I have to get it back up again and start over. That's what the enemy does to us in our lives, isn't it? He tries to be very subtle and if we're not alert, if we're not looking, we're not going to notice and see the things that can be impacting us and hurting us.

In the second chapter of Song of Solomon the woman reminds the man that they cannot let the little foxes come in and destroy their vineyard, representing their love and relationship. She realized that it was the little things that could ruin their love.

I ask you, "What are the little "foxes" or the little things in your life that you haven't been noticing, but are hindering your relationship with God?" Ask the Lord to reveal to you what those little things are. Maybe it's an integrity issue. Maybe you're watching things you shouldn't be watching. Maybe you're beginning to speak negatively about people that you shouldn't be and it's hindering relationships. Whatever it is, I would ask you to take it before the Lord, ask him to help you overcome it and begin fresh. Don't let the little foxes get in and destroy your vineyard.

Ask Yourself: What are the little things keeping me from God?

The Weather Patterns of Life

Bible Reading: Hebrews 13:8; John 16:33; Psalm 34:19

Changing weather patterns remind me of life. One day it's sunny and beautiful and the next day it's rainy, windy and cold. Life goes that way too sometimes.

The course of your life can change in an instant. Issues can come out of left field and completely change your forecast. But while life changes as quickly as the weather, our Lord Jesus Christ never changes. Hebrews 13:8 says, "Jesus Christ the same yesterday, and today, and for ever." Isn't it comforting to know that while everything else in life seems to change Jesus doesn't? We can always count on Him to be with us in life's storms.

So what kind of a storm are you facing? Is it financial, physical, mental or spiritual? Perhaps it involves a relationship. Everyone faces troubles that manifest themselves every day. But the Lord is always faithful to deliver you from them all. Jesus never said that following Him would make your life easy. On the contrary, in John 16:33, Jesus says, "In the world ye shall have tribulation: but be of good cheer; I have overcome the world."

If there's a changing weather pattern going on in your life right now, say this prayer, "Lord you know what I'm going through and how I should handle this situation. I'm putting my faith and trust in you." Finally, in Psalm 34:19 we read, "Many are the afflictions of the righteous: but the Lord delivereth him out of them all." Hang on to His promise that He will deliver you as you stay close to Him.

Ask Yourself: Do I panic when the storms roll in or do I have confidence that the Lord is with me even in the midst of it?

Taking the Right Road

Bible Reading: Proverbs 3:5-6; James 1:5

Robert Frost wrote a poem about two roads that diverged in a yellow wood. The poem is called *The Road Not Taken*. In the poem, Frost describes how he looked down each road as far as he could and tried to determine which road was best for him before he continued his journey. At the end of the poem he says, "I took the road less traveled by and that has made all the difference." This poem is about much more than deciding which road to take on a hike through the woods. It is about making an important life decision and how that decision can radically alter the rest of your life.

I think we have all thought about some of the major decisions we made years ago. If you're like me you have wondered how different your life would be if you had made a different choice. Some of the questions I ask myself are: What if I had married someone other than my wife? What if I had gone to a different college or chosen a different career path? What if I decided to take a different job? Life decisions require a great deal of wisdom. If you want to make the best decision you need to stay close to the Lord and seek His wisdom. Proverbs 3:5-6 tells us that we need to trust in the Lord with all of our heart and not lean on our own understanding.

The next time you find yourself at a crossroad make sure you have God's wisdom. Don't make a hasty decision, but spend time in prayer and let God speak to you through His Word. When you do those two things you can confidently choose the best road for you!

Ask Yourself: Am I close enough to God to trust that He will give me the wisdom I need for life's biggest decisions?

What is Your Worth?

Bible Reading: Matthew 10:29-31

Have you ever had one of those days when you just didn't believe you were worth much? I want to make sure you know that you are valuable. You might be sitting there right now feeling pretty low, not thinking you're worth much. You may not feel anybody cares about you or you feel alone in the world. Let me assure you that to God, you are of great value.

In Matthew, the tenth chapter, the Bible tells us that a sparrow does not fall to the ground without God knowing about it. It goes on to say that you are more valuable than many sparrows. Incredibly enough, it mentions even the very hairs on your head are numbered!

Just outside my office window is a bird feeder that is a true joy to watch. I have so many different birds that stop in for their breakfast or a midday snack. I can sit and watch these birds all day. (Okay, I promise, I do work a little!) It's incredible to stop and think that out of all the many birds that eat at my feeder, God monitors each one of them. And if

He cares about each of them, how much more does He care about you?

You think sometimes nobody's watching. You think sometimes you're in this by yourself, but you're not. God is closely watching you; he even knows your hair count. (Okay, I concede it's getting easier each year for God to keep mine counted.)

Please hear me loud and clear today that you are of such great value to God's kingdom. He cares for you so much and loves you immeasurably. Don't lose sight of that. Don't sit there and have a pity party. Recognize your value and start thanking the Lord for how much He loves you; how much He cares about you. Live your life today with the knowledge that God sees you as somebody with great worth.

Ask Yourself: Can I acknowledge my worth to God today?

God Already Knows What We Need

Bible Reading: Matthew 11:28-30

Do you have a relationship with Jesus? I'm not talking about having religion. It's not about a building or legalism or rules. It's about a personal relationship with someone to whom you can talk to as a friend. Jesus Christ is the best friend you will ever have. He's the Lord and Savior of the world, but He's also your friend and He wants to communicate with you daily. He wants to have a personal relationship with you. The way you do that is by praying, speaking to Him as if He was sitting in front of you and telling Him what is going on in your life.

God already knows what's happening in your life but He wants to hear it from you. He invites you to have an intimate relationship with Him. He wants you to tell Him about your struggles and your successes. God already knows what your needs are but He wants you have the faith to share them with Him. And your relationship goes both ways. When you speak to Him, He hears you. He knows your voice and He hears your requests. But He also knows what His will is for your life. Even as you speak to Him, listen for His voice. He speaks in many different ways and He answers every prayer according to His will. In Matthew 11:28 we read, "Come unto me, all ye that labour and are heavy laden, and I will give you rest."

Are there things going on in your life where decisions need to be made? Have a talk with Jesus. Tell him what's on your heart. Tell Him about the burdens you're bearing and the decisions you have to make. God already knows what you need but He loves to hear it from you.

Ask Yourself: Am I honest with Jesus and myself about each and every situation in my life?

Today is the Day! Rejoice!

Bible Reading: Ephesians 5:16; Psalm 118:24; 2 Corinthians 6:2

Have you ever walked into a restaurant and realized how many people are on their cell phones? I have often observed two people sitting across from each other interacting with their phones but ignoring each other! Sadly, many people don't know how to be "present" in today's world of technology.

It is so easy to let our phones control our lives. When I wake up in the morning my phone starts "pinging" as messages and notifications start coming in. I have to leave the phone alone so I can spend alone time with God. If I don't start my day in His presence then my day never goes right.

In Ephesians 5:16 we read, " Redeeming the time, because the days are evil." Those words ring true today. As Christians, we are called to reach out to others and help them in any way we can. But we have to be present. We have to spend time with them face to face.

When my late wife, Beth, was battling stage 4 cancer I

learned just how precious time was. We have a sitting room in our home where Beth loved to sit and enjoy her morning cup of coffee. When I would walk by she would pat the couch and say, "Come sit and have coffee with me." Many times I would tell her I was just too busy. However, once she received the stage 4 cancer diagnosis my priorities changed. From that time on, I always sat and had coffee with her and I would give anything to be able to do it again.

There is a popular saying which is a revision of a caption by cartoonist Bill Keane. It says, "Yesterday is history. Tomorrow is a mystery. But today is a gift. That is why it is called the present." How awesome is that! God gives us a new gift every 24 hours. He offers us a new start and another chance to redeem the time!

Ask Yourself: Am I spending my time wisely or am I being controlled by my phone or my computer?

Do You Doubt?

Bible Reading: Mark 9:17-27; Luke 5:1-7

I want to have more faith. I want to believe for what God can do in my life but invariably doubt overtakes me and then I feel guilty. Maybe you do the same thing. We need to know that God works despite our doubts.

There's a Bible story in Mark 9:17-27 about a man who had a son who had frequent seizures. He came to Jesus and asked for Jesus to do something if he could. He appeared to be questioning whether Jesus really could do *anything*. Jesus told him in verse 23, "If thou canst believe, all things are possible to him who believeth." Immediately the man cried out in verse 24, "Lord, I believe; help thou my unbelief." Unfortunately, that's the way I am far too many times. How about you? I believe. I have faith. Yet, I need help to believe because my doubt keeps creeping in. Well, the result of this story was God understood and healed the man's son.

Another great story regarding doubt is found in Luke 5:1-7. It involved Peter and the disciples. Jesus had just finished preaching and asked the disciples to get into the boat, push off from shore and throw out their nets. In verse 5, Peter said, "Master, we have toiled all the night, and have caught nothing: nevertheless at thy word I will let down the net." That doesn't sound like a lot of confidence in Jesus does it? Peter was full of doubt. The past told him there would be no fish.

Jesus knew something Peter didn't know. Jesus had already begun to send that school of fish to where the boat was even though Peter couldn't see it. The story ends with their nets so full of fish they could hardly pull them in. In fact, there were so many fish that the boat began to sink.

Don't focus on your doubts, but on the faith you have. God said if you have faith like a mustard seed you can do anything. Focusing on your faith and not your doubts allows God to do what He needs and wants to do in your life.

Ask Yourself: Will I allow my faith to replace my doubt today?

The Demons Know Who
Jesus Is. Do You?

Bible Reading: Matthew 8:28-33, Revelation 3:20

Do you know Jesus? It's a pretty simple question. Many people know *of* Jesus, but they don't actually know Him. Some think He was an enlightened teacher. Others think He was a prophet. There are some who think He was just an imaginary person and not a historical figure. If you fall into one of these categories then you don't really know Him. Matthew 8:28-33 tells us that even the demons knew that Jesus was the Son of God. That is why they feared Him.

Isn't it interesting that the demons recognized Jesus as the Son of God, yet the religious leaders of His time didn't? They constantly criticized Him. They didn't like that He spent time with undesirable people like prostitutes and thieves. They chastised Him for performing miracles on the Sabbath. They cried "Blasphemy!" when He said that He was one with the Father. They didn't recognize who He really was because they couldn't get past their preconceived ideas about how He should act and speak.

Jesus wants you to know who He is. He doesn't want you to just know about Him. He wants you to truly know Him. In Revelation 3:20 Jesus says, "Behold I stand at the door, and knock: if any man hear my voice, and open the door, I will come into him, and will sup with him and he with me." Jesus wants you to really know Him. He loves you and He wants to have a relationship with you. He wants to call you a friend.

If you want to get to know someone, you spend time with them. You talk to them and you listen to them. Jesus speaks to us today through the Word of God and the Holy Spirit, and we speak to Him through prayer. If you really want to know Jesus, this should be a part of your daily routine.

Ask Yourself: Do I simply know about Jesus or do I really know Him personally?

Step out of the Boat!

Bible Reading: Matthew 14:25-31

There are lots of famous walks in the Bible. The children of Israel walked through the wilderness for forty-years before arriving at the Promised Land. There was Joshua with his famous seven- day walk around the city of Jericho before the wall came down. Abraham had a very difficult walk up Mount Moriah when he thought he was going to have to sacrifice Isaac. But perhaps the most famous walk of all time only lasted a few seconds. It was when Peter got out of a boat and walked on water to come to Jesus.

In Matthew 14:25, we read that Jesus walked on the sea toward the boat that carried the disciples during the fourth watch of the night (approximately 3 a.m.) When the disciples saw Him they were filled with fear. Jesus quickly called out to them and told them not to be afraid. Peter was skeptical and said, in verse 28, "Lord, if it be thou, bid me to come unto thee on the water." You have to admire Peter's momentary courage. When He saw the Lord walking on the water, he thought that he could do it too. Jesus told him to come and the Bible says that Peter actually walked on water. But then something happened that caused him to lose his confidence. He took his eyes off Jesus and looked at his circumstances. He quickly realized that the wind was wild and fear gripped him. At this point, his faith wavered and he began to sink. But Jesus came to the rescue and caught him.

As long as Peter focused on Jesus he was good. He was actually doing something that is humanly impossible. He had his eyes on Jesus but then he lost his focus. He noticed the wind blowing very hard and he let fear creep in. Is God asking you to do something that you think is impossible? Remember, with God all things are possible. Your job is to get out of the boat and trust in the Lord. God wants you to leave your safety net and dare to trust Him to do great things through you. But regardless of your circumstances always keep your eyes fixed on your Savior!

Ask Yourself: Am I living my life the safe way because I don't really believe I can do something extraordinary? Are my eyes fixed on Jesus?

The Key to Happiness

Bible Reading: I Timothy 6:6-8; Galatians 6:4

Have you gone through those periods of time when you're just unhappy and sometimes you don't even know why? One thing that typically brings us a sense of unhappiness is that of comparison. Mark Twain says that comparison is the death of joy. If we look around there's always going to be somebody smarter, more talented, better looking and somebody with more hair. If we play the comparison game, it's easy to get down, be unhappy and lack contentment.

The Bible tells us contentment is the key to happiness. Listen to this scripture in I Timothy 6:6-8. It says, "But godliness with contentment is great gain. For we brought nothing into this world, and it is certain we can carry nothing out. And having food and raiment let us be therewith content." God is reminding us that our needs are being met, so we have no reason to not be happy and content. If you are, you have wrong expectations and focus for your life.

You've heard it said how social media has literally depressed the current generation. Many of us compare our lives with others while we focus on the routine of our lives. How can we compete with the highlight reels of other people's lives that we see on social media? It's not even a fair comparison. So if you're doing it, stop!

Galatians 6:4 tells us, "But let every man prove his own work, and then shall he have rejoicing in himself alone, and not in another." I encourage you to do your best in whatever you do today. If you do that, there is no reason for you to be unhappy or dissatisfied.

Do you want to be happy? Then don't compare yourself to someone else. Acknowledge that your needs are being met. Do the best you can and leave the rest to God. Allow the joy and the happiness that only He can bring radiate through your life today.

Ask Yourself: Will I choose to be happy today?

Do You Ever Feel Like Your Faith Is Being Tested?

Bible Reading: James 1:2-12; I Peter 1:6-8

Do you ever feel like your faith is being tested? Have there been times when you have said, "Oh Lord no, not again?" Or, "Why am I going through this?" We all go through trials that test our faith. When things are going bad you might hear someone say, "You've just got to have faith!" Guess what? They are absolutely right! In James 1:2-12, the Bible tells us about faith and how we are to endure through trials. It also tells us that we're supposed to ask for wisdom and to be humble and bold in our faith. Verses 2-4 tells us "My brethren, count it all joy when ye fall into divers temptations; Knowing this, that the trying of your faith worketh patience. But let patience have her perfect work, that ye may be perfect and entire, wanting nothing."

My mom was a great woman of faith. She was 90 years old when she passed away a couple of years ago. During her last couple of years, she spent more time in the hospital than out.

Her faith, however, remained strong through it all. I called her every time she went back in and asked, "Mom what's going on?" She would always say, "I don't know, but God has me here to speak to someone and I have to figure out who that person is." I loved her attitude! She believed that she was going in to speak to someone. She was convinced that God was using her broken body to minister to someone else. Her faith told her that God put her there for someone else and that He was going to do a mighty work in their life as she prayed for them.

Faith is powerful and when you see God working through you to help someone else it brings you great joy! Put your faith in God and believe in Him wholeheartedly. Look for His purpose in all things.

Ask Yourself: Do trials and tribulations work to weaken my faith or strengthen it?

What Was The Significance Of Jesus Turning Water Into Wine?

Bible Reading: John 2:1-11

What was the significance of Jesus turning water into wine? In the Bible, John 2:1-11, you'll find the story of this miraculous event.

Jesus, his mother, Mary, and his disciples were at a wedding in Cana of Galilee. Mary told the servants to do whatever Jesus instructed them to do. After the servants filled the stone jugs with water as Jesus commanded, He asked them to draw some water back out of the jug and present it to the master of the banquet. The master then went to the bridegroom and told him that he was impressed because everyone brings out the best wine first and then the cheaper wine. However, this bridegroom brought out the best wine last. Jesus had changed the water into the best wine! When the servants simply obeyed Christ's command, a miracle took place.

What I find most significant about this miracle is the difference between water and wine. Water is important because it sustains life. But wine is alive! If you talk to any wine vintner they will tell you that wine is a living thing that continues to age. That's why a wine sommelier will decant a young bottle of wine to expose it to oxygen. This quickens the aging process and makes the wine ready to consume.

The symbolism in this miracle, as I see it, is that you are the glass of water. When you accept Christ into your life, you're inviting His Spirit to dwell in you. His Spirit changes you and you become like new wine. When this happens people see the difference. They see Christ in you and hear Christ through you because you have His Spirit living in you. Something that was once just plain water is now fine wine. I believe that is why Christ chose this for His first miracle. Just like He changed the water into fine wine, He wants to change you into a beautiful vessel that He can use to bring others into His kingdom.

Ask Yourself: Have I asked God to transform me into all that He wants me to be?

It's Our Choice!

Bible Reading: Philippians 4:8

A couple of nights ago, I was trying to get to sleep. I usually fall asleep right away. I was tossing and turning. My mind was battling with some of the things I had said throughout the day that I realized I shouldn't have said, or at least could have said differently. I was riddled with frustration and guilt as it rolled over and over in my mind. Then, I thought about what people had said in response. I just couldn't get to sleep and I was going back and forth and then finally told myself, "Wait, wait, wait, stop right there! Why am I letting myself continue to think these thoughts?"

It is my choice as to what I think about. Nobody makes me think anything. I am choosing to think about those thoughts and be frustrated and be mad at myself and feel guilty. That is not benefiting me. It's not benefiting anybody else and I'm losing sleep.

I told myself, "I'm not going to do this anymore. I'm going to intentionally think about something else." I began to think about God and what He had done for me that day; all His blessings; all the goodness that He's shown me. My mind began to shift. It would drift back some at first, but as I began to focus more on God and all of His blessings, the negative thoughts faded away. I quickly dropped off to sleep.

I encourage you to take responsibility for your thoughts and your actions. No one else is making you do anything. It is your choice. Paul tells us in Philippians if we want the peace of God in our lives, we need to think on things that are true, honest, just, pure, lovely, of good report, virtuous and praiseworthy.

May your challenge today be to make your thoughts and actions line up with God's Word.

Ask Yourself: What will I allow my mind to dwell on today?

Is The Rain Nourishing You Or Destroying You?

Bible Reading: Matthew 5:45

Rain can be both welcomed and despised. It can be both good and bad. You can read in the Bible where rain has helped. It is essential for the farmers and the land to have rain at certain times of the year. Rain also brought destruction as in the days of Noah.

Rain can be a salvation or a curse to a farmer and the same is true in your life. We all go through periods of rain and storms in our personal lives. The effect they have on you is determined in large part by your attitude. Matthew 5:45 in the New Testament of your Bible says, "That ye may be the children of your Father, which is in heaven: for he maketh his sun to rise on the evil and on the good, and sendeth rain on the just and on the unjust." When the rains of life start falling, how do you adjust to it? Is it raining so much that you are getting caught up in the flood and washed away? Or is it nourishing you and helping you to grow? How you handle the rain in your life is totally up to you.

Rain can be life's circumstances that are dragging you down into depression. Perhaps certain friends are raining on you and causing confusion that could eventually lead to destruction in your life. Is the rain becoming a flood that's taking you under or is it nourishing you and helping you to grow in your knowledge of the Lord and in your walk with Jesus?

Rain can be something that's going to bless you or it can be something that will destroy you. When the rains come, you get to determine how you want them to be used in your life. You can use it for nourishment and growth or you can let it take you away in a flood and run you down into a valley of destruction. The choice is yours!

Ask Yourself: Am I getting nourished from the rains in my life or are they destroying me?

Oh Happy Day!

Bible Reading: Psalm 32:1; Romans 8:1-2; John 10:10

How would you feel if you knew that someday you were going to have everything you ever wanted? What if you knew that you would never have to worry about money or bills ever again? If I told you that the richest man in the universe was going to adopt you and take care of you and your family forever would you believe me? The fact is that if you know Jesus as your personal Savior and you have asked Him to forgive you of your sins, then all of this and more awaits you for all eternity! You are going to spend forever in heaven! This should make you very happy indeed!

In 1967 the Edwin Hawkins Singers recorded an 18th century hymn called *Oh Happy Day*. The first verse of that song repeats the words "Oh Happy Day" four times followed by "When Jesus Washed" six times, and it ends with "He washed my sins away!" I love that song! It is a song of celebration and it should fill every Christian's heart with pure joy.

Jesus has saved us from our sins. He paid the ultimate price on the cross and offers us the gift of eternal life forever! You and I can live in heaven with God and all of his saints for all eternity.

Franklin Graham spoke about his father, Billy Graham, at the latter's funeral. He said that his father had thought about heaven, preached about heaven and he wrote about heaven. Now he had taken his final journey to heaven. I know that Jesus greeted him and said, "Well done thou good and faithful servant." Can you imagine what a happy day that was for him? That day is coming for all of us, and that should make us very happy indeed!

Ask Yourself: Are you a truly happy person? Have you asked Jesus to forgive your sins?

Why Do You Doubt?

Bible Reading: Matthew 14:22-33

I'm sure you've heard the story of Jesus walking on the Sea of Galilee during a storm. Peter chose to step over the side of the boat and begin to walk on the water to Jesus. He looked down, began to sink and Jesus saved him. In Matthew 14:31, Jesus said to Peter, "O thou of little faith, wherefore didst thou doubt?" So many times we read that as a reprimand from Jesus, scolding him for a lack of faith.

I don't think Jesus was reprimanding as much as encouraging Peter. He was saying, "Oh, man, you almost did it! Just a little less doubt and a little more faith and you could have come right out to me!"

God presents opportunities every day for us to build our faith. That's what He did for Peter that night. The other disciples had the opportunity as well, but it was Peter that made the effort. It was Peter that chose to step out. Jesus didn't condemn him and He doesn't condemn you. He just prodded Peter along like He does to you and me. He was saying, "Don't you realize that when you're with me, together we can do the impossible. We can do incredible things!" That night was a steppingstone in Peter's faith building journey.

I think Jesus was just encouraging Peter, and He's going to do the same for you. Every one of us has daily opportunities to step out of the boat and start walking on the water. I challenge you to look for those faith-building moments today. Don't expect condemnation when you fail, but expect God to encourage you. Expect him to say, "I know you can do it! You CAN deepen this faith journey! We CAN do so much together! You CAN have fearless faith!" I believe that for you, that as God gives you opportunities to build your faith, you will step out and do it.

Ask Yourself: What faith building challenge am I going to meet through God's encouragement today?

Are You Heeding the Warning Signs?

Bible Reading: Proverbs 16:25; Psalm 32:8

Have you ever become so enamored with someone that you found yourself following them instead of God? Or perhaps you are so driven to succeed on your job that you have placed that as a priority over following the Lord. Whomever or whatever you have put ahead of God is leading you down the wrong path. If that is the case you need to change the direction you are headed in today!

I have heard the story of a man who was driving his car in a torrential downpour. Suddenly, he saw a man running toward him down the middle of the road waving his arms and yelling for him to stop. At first the driver thought the man was crazy and he was afraid to stop. However, the man was not moving off the road until the car screeched to a stop. When the driver rolled down his window, the man told him that the bridge on the road just ahead had collapsed and that if he kept going he would drive over a cliff and into the raging river below.

It is not God's plan for you to drive your life off a cliff. He gives you warning signs. If you look at your life honestly and pray for wisdom God will reveal to you when you are on the wrong road. He's your heavenly Father and as His child He wants you to go in the right direction with your life. Maybe He is speaking to you through this devotion right now. Heed God's warning before it is too late. The Bible tells us in Proverbs 16:25, "There is a way that seemeth right unto a man, but the end thereof are the ways of death."

God has a blueprint for your life and He is continually looking after you. He wants to lead you in the right direction. Choose to listen to God today and ask Him to lead you down the right road. Ask Him to grant you the courage to change your direction before it is too late.

Ask Yourself: Am I heading down a dangerous road that could lead to disaster?

Are You Numbering Your Days?

Bible Reading: Hebrews 9:27; Psalm 90:12; Romans 8:1

Billy Graham once said, "When a man is fully prepared to die then he is fully prepared to live." His words ring true. In Hebrews 9:27, we are told that we only die once. We don't come back and relive our lives over and over again until we get it right. We only have one chance. David wrote in Psalm 90:12, "So teach us to number our days that we may apply our hearts unto wisdom." In other words, we need to consider that our life is short and we need to make good use of our time! The wonderful thing is that once we ask God to forgive us of our sins by accepting what Jesus did for us on the cross we are no longer condemned. We are actually freed from the law of sin. We are truly free!!!

Let's face it. The death rate in the world today is 100%. None of us will get out of here alive. Thankfully, our souls will live on eternally with God in heaven if our sins are forgiven! Don't take a chance with your salvation. Many people don't believe that a loving God would send anyone to hell. The truth is He doesn't send anyone to hell. People choose to accept Him and the gift of salvation or they reject Him. Rejecting the Lord is taking a pretty big gamble.

My wife, Beth, was not afraid to die. In her last days, she told us that she was sad to leave us, but not afraid. She knew where she was going. God gave her glimpses of heaven and she told us it was beautiful. When she took her last breath on earth she took her first breath in heaven. She graduated from this life into the next and she was ready to go. Graduation day is coming!

Ask Yourself: Am I ready for my Graduation Day from earth? If I were to die today do I know that I'm going to heaven? You can be sure by asking Jesus to forgive you of your sins right now.

Is Your Life Out of Control?

Bible Reading: Isaiah 40:29-31

Do you feel like your life is out of control? Do you feel like you are always just responding to somebody else, always fulfilling responsibilities that you've been given? Maybe it's to your children. Maybe it's to your spouse. Maybe it's to work. Maybe it's to an ailing parent. Maybe it's to a handicapped child. Whatever it is, God knows and he understands what you're going through. Sometimes life feels hopeless. Sometimes it feels like you're never going to see the end and you are exhausted.

I've got good news for you! Isaiah 40:29-31 tells us "He giveth power to the faint; and to them that have no might he increaseth strength. He goes on to say in verse 30, "Even the youths shall faint and be weary, and the young men shall utterly fall: and now the 31ˢᵗ verse which says, "But they that wait upon the Lord shall renew their strength; they shall mount up with wings as eagles; they shall run and not be weary; and they shall walk and not faint."

Maybe that's you today. Maybe your life feels like it's out of control and hopeless. Maybe you're exhausted and see no hope of change. The Bible tells us to wait on the Lord. He will renew your strength. That promised day is coming! You're going to "mount up like an eagle". You will get through the challenges you're facing today. He's got power for you. He has strength for you. Be encouraged and renew your hope. God sees exactly what you're going through. He knows what you're feeling right now. He's got better days ahead. We've all heard the saying, "This too shall pass." It's true!

It's not going to go on forever, but even in your weakness he will give you strength. Hang on to that. It's not hopeless. God's right there with you. He wants to strengthen you and encourage you and give you the power you need to get through today. And then He'll be right there to do it again for you tomorrow.

Ask Yourself: What "out of my control" situation am I facing today that requires God's power and strength?

When You Need To Forget

Bible Reading: 2 Corinthians 5:17; Psalm 103:12

Have you ever asked yourself, "How can God forgive me when I can't even forgive myself?" Even though you've asked Jesus to forgive you of your sins, you still feel that He didn't. You still feel guilty.

Satan loves to bring up the past and use it against you. He doesn't want you to believe that you have really been forgiven. However, according to God's Word, the past is gone. When you accepted Christ into your life, the past was forgiven. Your slate was wiped clean. What was once stained is now white as snow. But Satan wants you to question your forgiveness by putting doubts in your mind. The Bible tells us in II Corinthians 5:17, "Therefore if any man be in Christ, he is a new creature: old things are passed away; behold, all things are become new." The past is gone. It's time to move on and live a new day. It's not about the past anymore, it's about your future in Christ.

In Psalm 103:12 we read, "As far as the east is from the

west, so far hath He removed our transgressions from us." It doesn't matter what is in your past. When you asked Christ to come into your life and to forgive you, He washed you clean. The sins you openly admitted and asked forgiveness for are now as far as the east is from the west. In other words, Jesus will never haunt you with your past.

Seek God for the plan He has for you in your future; determine how you're going to live your life from this day forward because your past has been forgiven. If you have sincerely asked Christ for forgiveness then you have been justified. I heard a preacher once say, "When I am justified it's just as if I'd never sinned." Don't let the devil put thoughts into your head that will stop you from growing in the Lord. Don't live your life looking in the rear view mirror when your future lies ahead.

Ask Yourself: Have I let go of the past and am I moving ahead with my life in the glorious light of God's forgiveness?

Powerful Yet Personal

Bible Reading: Psalm 19:1; Matthew 19:26; Psalm 139:14-16

When was the last time you looked up into the sky on a really clear night and were filled with a sense of awe and wonder? It is impossible not to be when you see hundreds and hundreds of stars and realize that most of those stars are hundreds of light years away. That means moving at the speed of light (about 186,000 miles per second!) it would take hundreds of years to reach them. The furthest star to the unaided eye is a little over 4000 light years away. Recent estimates put our universe at a diameter of 93 billion light years! That just boggles the mind! Obviously, the Creator of the Universe is extremely powerful!

On the other hand, when you study the human body and understand that it is made up of approximately 37.2 trillion cells you realize how infinitesimal a cell is. God created the incredibly vast universe and He created us from incredibly small cells. We read about God's power in Psalm 19:1 and Matthew 19:26. The heavens declare His handiwork and nothing is impossible for Him. However, in Psalm 139:14-16 we read about how His eye was on us as He formed us in the womb. He knew us before we were born. God cares about the intimate details of our lives.

It is truly amazing to me that the Creator of the vast universe cares about the details in my life. He is powerful and personal. He cares about you and me so much that He came to earth and died on the cross so that we can live with Him forever if we simply ask Him into our hearts.

Ask Yourself: Do I believe that there is any problem in my life that the Creator of the Universe cannot solve?

Faith Over Fear

Bible Reading: Ephesians 6:16; Hebrews 11:6

The Bible is full of scripture on faith and it's importance to our walk with the Lord. You can't be a Christian without it. In the sixth chapter of Ephesians, Paul tells us about the pieces of our spiritual armor that we put on to fight our spiritual battle. It says in the 16th verse, "Above all, taking the shield of faith". Out of everything you should wear for your spiritual battle, faith is the key.

To build a strong case for the importance of faith, Hebrews 11:6 says, "But without faith it is impossible to please him." Obviously you want to please God but you can't do it without faith. Why would that displease God? Well, if you don't have faith what do you have? The opposite of faith is fear, anxiety and worry. If that's what you are dealing with today, then you're lacking faith. God wants to help you develop that faith.

There's nothing good that comes out of worry, anxiety and fear. It hurts you. It hurts your body. It hurts your relationships and destroys your faith. The Bible calls it sin. Worry is sin. So if that's you today, turn the worry and the anxiety over to God and seek faith. I know it's not as easy as it sounds when you're worried, but if you focus on Him your worries will begin to fade away and your faith will be stronger.

When you worry, you're basically telling God that you don't believe He has the power and the ability to take care of you. What an embarrassing message to send to God. The Bible says in Luke to make up your mind not to worry. That's your challenge today. Make up your mind now before anything happens and before there's something big to worry about. Make up your mind not to worry. Replace your worry with faith that only God can give and He will help you.

Ask Yourself: Can I make it through a worry-free day?

Don't Live in the Rearview Mirror

Bible Reading: Isaiah 43:18-19

It would be pretty dangerous to drive a car with your eyes constantly looking in the rearview mirror. You need to be focused on what's going on in front of you the majority of the time when you are driving. The same is true in life. If you really want to move forward and accomplish things, your eyes need to be looking at the present and the future. Are you holding on to something from your past that is keeping you from moving forward? Is there something that is keeping you from living a complete life? Sometimes when you hold onto something or someone from the past it can drag you down and get you off course from where you need to be going. It can be family, work, personal relationships or financial obligations just to name a few.

In Isaiah 43:18-19 of the Bible we read, "Remember ye not the former things, neither consider the things of old. Behold, I will do a new thing; now it shall spring forth; shall ye not know it? I will even make a way in the wilderness, and rivers in the desert." God is saying to forget the things of the past. Let go of whatever it is that is holding you back and diverting you away from the direction you should be going. Follow Jesus and put your faith and trust in Him.

But how do you do that? By talking to the Lord daily. Pray this prayer, "Father I trust you with my future. I'm letting go of what's holding me back. I know you have something better planned and that you have a path already designed just for me. Thank you for hearing my prayer. In Jesus name, Amen." God hears your prayers and He will open up the pathway for you to follow Him. Remember when you are holding onto something tight your hand is closed and not open to receive what God wants to put into it today.

Ask Yourself: What am I holding on to that is keeping me from experiencing something new and better that God has for me?

About the Authors

Dan Wheeler - Dan has an extensive background in broadcast communications, having worked in radio and television for over 40 years. His broadcast journey included disc jockey, on-air sportscaster, news director, senior producer and production company owner. He hosted and produced a variety of programming that garnered him seven *Religion in Media* awards as well as several local *Emmy* Award nominations.

In 1988, Dan became a prime-time television host with the QVC network. He retired at the end of 2017 after a 29-year career in that role.

Dan lives in Pennsylvania and lost his loving wife, Beth, to cancer in 2015. He is a proud father of two daughters, Kirstyn and Kelsey, and grandfather to Cole, Gavin and Brooke.

Brian Roland – Brian is a 35-year entertainment industry veteran. As a Producer/Director, he has won 2 Emmy Awards and 17 Angel Awards. He has worked various positions, including launching 8 International Networks for the Discovery Channel International, General Manager of

Georgia Dome Productions, Director of Network Operations and Director of Business Development at Crawford Communications.

Brian also worked in the film industry and has been successful with on-air presenting, production, operations, business development and sales.

Brian lives in California with his beautiful wife Debora and their two dogs.

Terry Steen – Terry is an ordained minister and has served in various church and ministry leadership roles for over 40 years. His various roles include Accounting Manager, Chief Financial Officer, Church Business Administrator and Executive Pastor.

For the last 20 years Terry has consulted with churches and pastors in the area of finances, budgeting and acquiring funds for ministry.

Terry lives in Florida with his lovely wife, Karen. He has one incredible daughter, Ashley, and three priceless grandchildren, Alison, Samuel and Bria.